ENCOURAGING WOR~~I~~ ... ~~IVE~~ PRAYER

"This book stirred my heart and commitment to pray for revival in our lives, churches and communities. What a compelling biblical exposition rooted in missional conviction and practical insight!"

~Mark Reynolds, *Vice President, Leadership Development, Redeemer City to City*

"There is no shortage of literature on prayer, so why the need to add another title? *Disruptive Prayer* fills an important gap. John takes the reader through the pages of Scripture and draws out a very practical guide to kingdom prayer. *Disruptive Prayer* is written to awaken a generation to the power, potential, and preeminence of prayer in the kingdom. The book is provoking and practical. It identifies the barriers of fear and idolatry that are not just holding us back as individuals but as communities, cities, and even nations. It just might disrupt your prayer life—in a good way!"

~Craig Kraft, *Executive Director, Outreach Canada*

"Solid and convicting. A biblical call for us to connect with our God."

~Tom Wood, *Author of Gospel Coach*

"As our ministry strategizes and plans for gospel renewal in the global cities of the world, I am often reminded that without prayer all of the best strategies and plans will not come to fruition. John reminds us that 'every kingdom movement starts with prayer.' The ministry of City to City has greatly benefited from the principles of *Disruptive Prayer* and have sharpened our focus as an organization around gospel-centered prayer."

~Steve Shakelford, *Executive Director, Redeemer City to City*

"Read this book, and read it again. There are books on prayer, and then there is this one. Filled with prophetic insights distilled from a lifetime spent on the front lines of mission, this little book is packed with rich theological reflection, careful biblical insights, and practical application. It is not another book on prayer—it is an invitation to another way of living. It is disruptive, as Jesus was. Read it and be changed."

~Dan MacDonald, *Senior Minister, Grace Toronto Church*

"John's writing is Spirit-Led and laser-focused on the mission of renewal and revival in the church. *Disruptive Prayer* is an apt title as this kind of praying disrupts our comfortable, consumeristic lives; disrupts sleepy churches; and ultimately will disrupt the spiritual forces of evil in the heavenly realms. May God use it to 'disturb the comfortable and to comfort the disturbed.'"

~Mark Burch, *North America Director for Church Planting, Multiply*

"*Disruptive Prayer* is a resounding call for all Christians to contend for the kingdom of God in faith on their knees. Every page is a reminder that throughout the history of the people of God, prayer actually changes things; it disrupts the orders and systems of the world. If you hunger to see God's power at work in our cities, nations and world, then this book will equip you to be a part of what God is doing through His people when they pray."

~Stephen Mulder, *Associate National Director, Alpha Canada*

"This book goes for the heart! It also goes quickly to the real issues facing the church. It moves fast and yet it goes deep. John has uniquely identified the problems facing the contemporary church, but he also brings biblical ideas and truth so that we journeymen will have a workable tool that can be adapted to any group or church. I have seen two crippled churches move quickly to a new focus and practice of prayer."

~Terry Gyger, *Coordinator, LinX church renewal ministry, Emeritus Executive Director, Redeemer City to City*

"I have read numerous books on prayer. But the book you hold in your hand is the one that has affected me the most as an adult. It is deeply biblical and deeply practical at the same time. John takes us through the Scriptures as if leading an adventure in prayer. This is not a technique book or the "secrets to prayer" kind of book. I found myself praying my way through the book as if on a prayer walk and standing in the presence of the Father as if united with the ascended Christ. May his kingdom come!"

~Russ Simons, *Missionary kid, World Venture missionary to the Philippines and Asia, Consultant to World Evangelical Alliance on Prayer*

"Fervent prayer is one of the most powerful and overlooked tools in the Western Christian's arsenal. Packed with decades of pastoral insight, yet *Disruptive Prayer* doesn't merely offer a formula of how to pray; rather, it gives us the heart and philosophy behind why we must pray. John and his wife Caron have lived the deep reality that prayer is many things; a tool, an act of worship, an act of subversion, a culture shaper, but most of all a privilege for the people of God. Will we answer *Disruptive Prayer*'s call to avail ourselves more deeply of intimate communion with the God of the Universe?"

~K.A. Ellis, *Cannada Fellow for World Christianity,*
Reformed Theological Seminary

"This is a fresh view of prayer from a long-time faithful practitioner, placing it as an essential and strategic element in the progress of God's kingdom. One thinks of Paul, who at the end of describing the various pieces of Christian armor, ties them all together with prayer as the imperative, as if to say: 'This is the last and essential piece in the armor of God.'"

~Rev. Dr. Peter Jones, *Director, truthXchange,*
Adjunct Professor, Westminster Seminary California

"Every generation of the church needs a prophetic voice to rouse it from complacency. In picking up *Disruptive Prayer,* prepare to hear God calling you to a movement of prayer, revival, and renewal in our day! It is clear, compelling, and constructive."

~Connan Kublik, *Director Grace Network Canada,*
Church Planter, New City Church, Hamilton, Ontario, Canada

"Each year, we close nearly as many churches as we start. A majority of our existing congregations are plateaued or declining. And many of us feel like we don't know where to turn. I love what John Smed says to us in this kind of space: It is at just such moments that God often pours out a spirit of kingdom prayer on his people, prayer that leads to deep repentance, and amazing gospel advance through word and deed, such that our towns and cities and states and regions become different places, full of the rejoicing that comes with the presence of the kingdom of God."

~Paul Hahn, *Coordinator, Mission to North America*

"'We become what we pray.' This sentence alone, as contextualized in *Disruptive Prayer*, is disrupting my life and ministry so that I turn from what John describes as 'default prayers' focused on personal problems. It has inspired me to reimagine the place and power of prayer under Christ's ascension ministry and to expect a powerful and illuminating divine-human encounter. I'm still pondering the message that 'prayer increases our capacity for God.'"

~Preston Graham Jr., *Sr. Pastor, Christ Presbyterian Church, New Haven, Director, Mission Anabaino*

"I have read many books on prayer that are both informative and insightful. Books that make me want to take notes and keep reading. But John's book is counterintuitive. It, in fact, does not inspire more reading. Rather, it makes me want to stop reading, to set the book down—and pray 'Thy kingdom come.'"

~Al Breitcruz, *Salvation Army Team Leader Abbotsford, BC, Canada*

"Like the flashing stick-figure on my dash reminding me to buckle up before driving, *Disruptive Prayer* reminds me that prayer precedes any real advance of the gospel, and prayer is what sustains it. The biblical and historical evidence is there for us to see in John's book, and we need to heed the call to join in united prayer to partner with our Lord in his mission."

~Dan Rutherford, *Founder of The Activate Course*

"'Disruptive' means 'to interrupt the normal course or unity of.' A word most often attributed to the effect of new and emerging technologies on our culture. John aptly shows us how kingdom centered praying is the ultimate challenge to the status quo and current spiritually anemic climate of much of the Western church. It's a clarion call not to grab a hold of a prayer program but more of being awakened to be grabbed a hold of by the Spirit of prayer of supplication."

~Michael Ivancic, *Founder Grace on Bow outreach forum, Technology Senior Account Manager/Associate Pastor New City Church*

"God is calling the church in North America to rediscover the place and power of corporate prayer. John Smed gives voice to this call, as he unpacks the Scriptures, church history, and our present day need for the recovery of a movement of corporate prayer."

~Darin Pesnell, *Lead Pastor, Iron Works Church, Philadelphia*

"As the leader of a Christian, non-profit housing society, I am both encouraged and challenged by this call. to prayer The line in *Disruptive Prayer* proclaiming, 'corporate prayer is the soil in which vision from God grows from mustard seed to mighty plant, providing shade and shelter for many,' is an invitation to our organization to remain faithful in prayer and believe God for great things."

~Lee-Anne Michayluk, *CEO, More Than a Roof Housing Society*

"We pray that *Disruptive Prayer* will multiply the grace of God and mobilize the church worldwide over and over and over again."

~James Greenelsh, *International missions videographer*

"As a 30-something millennial who grew up in the church, I've heard all the cute formulas for 'super quick' post Bible study prayer (popcorn prayer, anyone?). This book is not one of them. Comprehensively gathering all the Bible's references to prayer, John explores a pattern that reveals corporate prayer as not just a last-reserve tool for revival, but the sign of revival itself."

~*Alexa Gilker,* screenwriter and playwright

"*Disruptive Prayer* has been born out of deep reflection on the word of God as well as years of ministry experience. Indeed, as John writes in his introduction, 'Every kingdom movement starts with prayer.'"

~Lloyd Kim, *Coordinator, Mission to the World*

"This book is both a challenge and a guide to the church to commit itself to prayer by drawing on the clear teachings of Scripture, and by a careful theological framework that shapes the basis, motives and purposes of prayer. I highly recommend it."

~Gene Haas, *Emeritus professor Redeemer College, Hamilton,Ontario, Canada*

"My most faith-challenging time began with four months of treatment for alcoholism and drug addiction. A few months into my recovery, I was blessed to be introduced to *Disruptive Prayer*. The foundation of my recovery had to be a no-holds-barred relationship with my Creator. *Disruptive Prayer* has inspired me to look deeply into all that my Savior has done for me and what my response to him should be."

~*Susan S.,* a woman God has delivered, restored, and is setting free

"*Disruptive Prayer* breaks down strongholds, conquers kingdoms, and obtains promises. A must read if you want your church, community, and nation changed."

~Rose Marie Miller, *author* From Fear to Freedom
Nothing Is Impossible With God

"Through the ages there have been volumes written on this topic. John's book *Disruptive Prayer* stands out as a gem. It is thorough, enlightening and filled with examples from history for today's leaders who want to keep growing in their understanding of prayer."

~Lorne Epp, *Founder, CEO, Executive Coach,
More Than A Roof Housing Society*

"I read *Disruptive Prayer* in the midst of a life as a mother, a member of my neighbourhood, and as a ministry worker—where the 'tyranny of the urgent' can too easily cloud my view of who God is and diminish the priority of prayer in my life. John paints a vivid picture of calling on God recaptured my vision for the greatness of God and renewed my conviction for kingdom-centered prayer."

~Peggy Porter, *Campus Minister, Power to Change*

"John's book *Disruptive Prayer* is written for such a time as this. He speaks with relevance to our generation. I was particularly convicted by the chapter on removing idols through kingdom prayer. As a result, I am spending more time in prayer and the Word of God and reduced dramatically wasting time on the Internet. I pray that many will read this book and be challenged to seek God in prayer."

~Axa Carnes, *Prayer Trainer, Teacher Trainer, ESL Teacher*

"*Disruptive Prayer* provides us with refreshing perspectives and encouraging testimonies how a movement of prayer can be used nowadays to continue the disruptive and transformative movement started by the Holy Spirit even from biblical times. I can feel the passion the author has for prayer, for the church, for the city and ultimately for God. Well-done."

~Edward Ng, *Elder Ottawa Chinese Alliance Church*

DISRUPTIVE PRAYER

The Movement Starts Here

John F. Smed

Prayer
Current
Navigating Life Through Prayer

Acknowledgements

I am thankful and indebted to gifted and dedicated co-laborers, Justine Hwang, Renée and Mark Reynolds, Anne Husak and James Greenelsh—who were faithful (and frank) with many helpful suggestions, edits and additions. They were among many who helped 'pray it forward' to completion. Thanks especially to my wife Caron, who constantly encourages me to sit down and write down the wonderful things God is teaching me about kingdom prayer.

Dedication

To those inspiring brothers and sisters who have learned to pray through adversity and turn consternation into intercession for their persecutors—EW and Deborah in China, Aliesky in Cuba and Jim, Daniel, Vijay and Ebenezer in India. No one moves ahead without great friends and co-laborers like Bert and Carole Gibson, Evan and Marilynn Bottomley, and my constant colleague, Tom Wood.

CONTENTS

Disruptive Prayer

The Purpose for Writing This Book

Our purpose for writing this book is simple: to issue a biblical call to prayer that fuels a prayer movement for kingdom advance throughout North America.

The outcome we seek, though simple, is anything but small-minded. It is our constant prayer that our Savior King might pour out his Spirit to revive his church and renew our cities and land. The first evidence of the coming of Christ's kingdom will be a deep transformation of the character and activity of the church. The result will be radical renewal of city life and restructuring of society in all its workings—indeed *disruptive* in the most wonderful sense of the word. There will be "joy in the city" when people hear and receive the good news (Acts 8:8). As believers gather in earnest and united prayer, the gates of the city will "open for them of its own accord." (Acts 12:5,10) As prayer relentlessly prevails against seen and unseen opposition, those who preach the gospel will once again be accused of turning "the whole world upside down." (Acts 17:6)

Nor is it a humble aim to imagine we can attain an intensive movement of kingdom prayer considering the current anemic state of the church when it comes to prayer. It seems fanciful to imagine the present inertia can be reversed and that the doldrums be replaced by the Spirit's mighty wind of prayer.

Indeed, respected church and mission analysts have argued that there is little likelihood of us experiencing a major advance of the kingdom in our context in the near future.

"...Church planting movements are unlikely to happen in our Western context within our generation." (Ed Stetzer and Daniel Im, Multiplication Today, Movements Tomorrow, 2016)

While these writers might provide an accurate description of our existing situation, the biblical narrative leaves little room for pessimistic predictions. In fact, in both Old and New Testaments we find that great revivals and attendant renewals are often quite literally "just a prayer away." It is in darkest times of decline, amid periods of stunning indifference to God's kingdom, that God often pours out a spirit of prayer and repentance that becomes an overwhelming tide of truth that converts hearts and heals nations (see 2 Chronicles 7:14, Zechariah 12:10-13:2).

Disruptive Prayer is a biblical, experiential study

The scarcity of sources other than the Bible throughout *Disruptive Prayer* is intentional. The biblical narrative concerning prayer and kingdom advance speaks for itself and speaks with unstoppable force and indisputable clarity. There is no great need for exegetical prowess or extra biblical endorsement when the Bible itself admits no exceptions to the argument that prayer is at the forefront in every case of church revival and urban renewal. Nothing can improve upon the biblical argument for the primacy and priority of prayer. When asked to defend the Bible, Charles Spurgeon retorted, "Defend the Bible? I would as soon defend a lion."

Disruptive Prayer is a biblical study, but it is not theoretical. We write as practitioners and to encourage practitioners. We have studied and practiced kingdom prayer in the context of urban mission for more than 30 years. This includes extensive and intensive involvement with the church in North America: planting two churches, one in city-center Vancouver; serving as church planting director of Mission to North America; and founding a Canada-wide church planting team, The Grace Network. We have worked for 30 years to insert kingdom prayer into movements and networks of church planting from which this current prayer ministry was formed. In order to devote all of our time and energy to fueling a movement of kingdom prayer, Prayer Current Ministries was formed in 2012. Since this time we have been involved in prayer discipleship throughout North America and Cuba, and more recently in India and China.

For these reasons, Disruptive Prayer is an experiential study. We have first-hand testimony that coheres with the biblical narrative concerning prayer and kingdom advance. With no end of failures and admitted weaknesses, we can say we have walked the talk when it comes to prayer and kingdom advance. We have seen the fruit and advance of prayer in evangelism and mission. With grief and sadness, we have also seen the poverty and performance orientation when mission is attempted without prayer at the center. The warnings of the first verse of Isaiah 30 ring true and describe a good deal of what often passes for kingdom mission: *"Ah, stubborn children,' declares the Lord, 'who carry out a plan, but not mine, and who make an alliance, but not of my Spirit, that they may add sin to sin..."* (Isaiah 30:1)

A thematic outline

Although *Disruptive Prayer* is a biblical study, we have
followed a thematic rather than biblical chronology. The
sequence and trajectory of the book begins with the prayer life
and teaching of Christ. From Christ's Spirit as the source, the
prayer practices and advances of the early church follow. From
praying believers begin the work of rebuilding and renewing
city and society.

In the first section of the book, *Kingdom Prayer Breaks In*, we
focus on the prayer life of Jesus. In Chapter 1, we discover that
prayer initiates every kingdom advance in Jesus' life. In Chapter
2, Jesus teaches his disciples then and now a lasting strategy
and pattern for prayer, which captures all the priorities of the
coming kingdom. In Chapter 3 we see Jesus come in storm and
fury to purify his people for prayer.

In the second section, *Kingdom Prayer Breaks Out*, we
encounter the awesome power of prayer in the newly formed
community of faith. In Chapter 4, we explore ascension
prayer. From Jesus' exalted place of ascension glory, he pours
out a Spirit of prayer. This prayer literally brings down gale
force winds, fire, and earthquake. In Chapter 5 we find that a
praying church is the agency God uses to multiply thousands of
converts and to overthrow the powers that subvert the religious
and political status quo. In Chapter 6 we learn how the apostle
Paul prayed with power to fuel a global movement. In Chapter
7 we explore the binary relationship between church revival and
city renewal that continues throughout history.

In the third section of the book, *Kingdom Prayer Breaks
Through*, we encounter the power of repentant prayer to revive
the church and renew the city. Chapter 8 outlines a pattern of
biblical and church history in which united prayer precedes
spiritual victory, overturns idols, and restores communities. In
chapter 9 we are challenged to discern the idols in our day and
time and to meet them head on with prayer. Chapter 10 unpacks

how prayer sustains personal piety and kingdom advance in the midst of captivity. In Chapter 11, church revival and city renewal meet in a prayer celebration of cosmic proportions.

Disruptive Prayer ends with a reflective study of Old and New Testament prayer visions, images that unite the major themes of the coming kingdom of God with the faithful and earnest practice of prayer. The cycle of birth and rebirth of the church is filled with pain and travail, and yet raging seas are navigated by a prayerful dependence on a sovereign God. Eventually the storm subsides as creation, church, and city find perfect wholeness in the New Jerusalem.

Defining a key term

Throughout the book we refer to several related terms—kingdom prayer, the coming kingdom, the advance and expansion of the kingdom— all of which beg for a clear definition of what is meant by the term kingdom. As one would expect, we have strong conceptions of what the term means. However, rather than attempting to supply a single or simple definition of kingdom, which would be impossible in our estimation, we have added into every chapter an important facet to one's overall understanding of the biblical concept of the kingdom of God—and more specifically, the coming of the kingdom. We intend that the overall call to prayer in *Disruptive Prayer* brings together several of the essential aspects of the coming of the kingdom in varied, inspiring ways. We can only hope that we do justice to the great adventure of what it means to serve the King of kings and Lord of lords and become part of Jesus' mighty work in bringing the kingdom of God into the hearts and lives of all people!

The reader will find that we use the term kingdom movement and prayer movement interchangeably; quite simply this is because there is no kingdom movement that is not fueled by prayer. At the same time, we find that concerted, united prayers of God's people initiate and permeate every advance of the kingdom.

We realize there are different, and even competing, conceptions of what the coming of the kingdom is about and therefore what constitutes kingdom prayer. Our argument goes against the grain of some prevailing thought on the subject. We have chosen not to enter into the fray to dispute on these matters for a few reasons.

For one, this study is not intended to be the last word on prayer. Prayer is as rich and varied a topic as is our relationship with Christ, and it's as deep as the Scriptures themselves. Every praying believer is experiencing the Spirit of God and learning important lessons about prayer that can benefit the entire church.

Secondly, we have not written this book to discourage anyone who prays in faith to Christ. Rather, we hope to strengthen all who pray and to add some helpful and important insights along the way.

Finally, if this book is not the last word on prayer, we are serious that it is the first word. It is our firm conviction that the biblical narrative supports our assertion that kingdom prayer has primacy and priority when it comes to kingdom advance—that every advance and expansion of God's kingdom begins and is fueled by prayer.

This is what we mean when we say that kingdom prayer is disruptive.

Not far from where our work of kingdom prayer began in Vancouver, British Columbia, lies the coastal region of Tofino, storm-ridden beaches consecrated to wave watching and surfing. On typical days six-foot waves steadily advance toward the shore. In stormy seasons, however, the waves often reach thirty and even forty feet, a stunning display of aquatic power that flings logs like twigs, lays waste to rickety piers, and dramatically reshapes the shoreline. For onlookers, it is a terrifying yet thrilling thing to behold.

As this book will attempt to demonstrate, the kingdom of God, like the waves he commands, is relentlessly advancing. God Almighty is shaping the world toward his intended destiny. At most times and places the progress is steady and barely noticed; the leaven and salt of the kingdom is doing its work. This might describe kingdom advance in the Western world. At other times and places, the kingdom surges forward with violent force, and the world-shaking forces of Pentecost are unleashed. Every person and place is buffeted by the advancing waves of spiritual upheaval. Both the church and the world are radically reshaped. We call this revival.

When the sea is stormy, small faith prefers to observe from the shore. Greater faith longs to dive in and feel the pounding surf. Small prayers stay focused on the safe and predictable. Great prayers love to explore the torrent of God's power and reclaim the embrace of his love.

Prayer is how we seize the power of the Spirit and enter the powerful surge of the coming kingdom. Prayer is disruptive, because the coming of the kingdom is disruptive. Apart from prayer we remain spectators on the shore. But as we engage in prayer, we are caught up in the thrilling adventure of the kingdom of God and discover the unfolding plan of Christ.

Every kingdom movement starts with prayer.

Author's notes

This call to prayer is rooted in a biblical study of the primacy and priority of prayer in Old and New Testament awakenings, and advances of the kingdom. Our labor and intent are that Disruptive Prayer honors the biblical call to prayer flowing from the biblical narrative and teaching itself.

Concerning sources

To allow scripture to speak for itself, we have made sparing references to secondary sources. I am familiar with a great deal of powerful writing on prayer and I am hugely indebted to several authors. I still drink deeply from the reformers. I discovered from their lives and writings that prayer was equal in priority to preaching. I heartily commend anything and everything written about prayer by Charles Spurgeon and Andrew Murray. More recent writers that have changed my prayer life forever include Jacques Ellul, Daniel Bloesch, D. A. Carson and James Houston.

I have also spent years studying and sitting under great teachers who are godly models of personal prayer as well as prayer for mission. For example, from the day I became a Christian, I experienced months of kingdom prayer discipleship under Edith Schaeffer of L'Abri Fellowship.

I have chosen to use the English Standard Version as it seems to capture the intent of the original languages in an accessible English translation.

References to Canada

As I attempt in prayer to diagnose the present state of church, city, and nation, in several places I make reference to Canada. As this is the place I am from, where I have ministered for most of my forty-five years as a Christian, and where I am most familiar with our church and society, I can be most confident making references to Canada in my analysis and assertions. For the sake of integrity and applicability, I want to be specific in my witness of the need for, and effect of, kingdom prayer.

However, with my wife and children, I lived for ten years in the U. S. and have been active in most parts of the county—I am confident that application to America's context will not be a difficult task for the reader. To our surprise, we find that our applications of the biblical call to and teaching about prayer are both needed and helpful in other global contexts as we have ministered extensively in Cuba, and more recently in India and China.

Disruptive Prayer

Kingdom Prayer Breaks In

Disruptive Prayer

CHAPTER I

The King Comes in Prayer

Jesus Imparts His Life of Prayer Through Presence, Teaching, and Example

A s we contemplate Jesus' life among us, a central observation emerges—that the King comes in prayer. Jesus lived a life of prayer. He navigated his life by prayer. He enjoyed uninterrupted fellowship with the Father. Through his prayers, Jesus called down from heaven infinite grace and power to inaugurate and advance the kingdom.

The king comes in prayer, and he brings prayer with him. By his life of prayer, his teachings on prayer, and his giving us a Spirit of prayer, Jesus births a praying people.

For a life of prayer, we find all we need in Jesus.

Jesus provides everything we need to ensure our constant communion with God. We not only have his example and teaching, but we also have his personal friendship, his mediation, and his presence in prayer.

Jesus offers each and every believer a prayer friendship.

Those who pray experience intimacy with Christ as he reveals his plans and purposes:

> *The servant does not know what his master is doing. I have called you friends, for all that I have heard from my Father I have made known to you...so that whatever you ask the Father in my name, he may give it to you.* (John 15:15,16)

True prayer is friendship prayer—friendship with Jesus.

Who doesn't need a good friend? A friend is someone you can always confide in. A friend is someone you can always rely on. Realizing that Jesus is your best and truest friend in prayer opens up a whole new world of confidence and adventure.

Jesus prays with and for us.

At present, even as we pray, Jesus as our mediator prays with and for us. He intercedes for his people on the basis of his finished work on the cross. This is an astounding truth and great blessing in prayer—we can cast aside guilt and doubt when we offer our prayers in the name of Jesus, *"Who is to condemn? Christ Jesus is the one who died—more than that, who was raised—who is at the right hand of God, who indeed is interceding for us."* (Romans 8:34)

Jesus purifies our prayers.

Our prayers are made acceptable in the mediatory work of Jesus. This image is found in Leviticus 16:12,13 and Revelation 8. As the incense of our prayers ascend to God, they are mixed with the burning coals of the altar, resulting in petitions that are fragrant, purified and pleasing to God:

> *And another angel came and stood at the altar with a golden censer, and he was given much incense to offer with the prayers*

of all the saints, rose before God from the hand of the angel,
and the smoke of the incense, with the prayers of the saints, rose
before God from the hand of the angel. (Revelation 8:3,4)

Each and every believer has confidence entering the most
holy presence of God through the blood sacrifice of Jesus.
Jesus carries us into heaven itself. This high-priestly work of
Christ brings a profound and enduring boldness to our prayers
(Hebrews 10:19-22).

This is what it means to pray in Jesus' name; as we pray, we
invoke the purifying merit of his mediatory work.

Jesus indwells us in his Spirit of prayer.

Lastly and wonderfully, in order that we might enjoy answer
upon answer to our prayers, Jesus gives each believer his Spirit
of prayer. Often, we do not know how to pray; the Holy Spirit
dwells deep within every believer and "groans" alongside us.
Often we do not know what to ask for, and the Holy Spirit
teaches us to pray the right thoughts and words:

Likewise, the Spirit helps us in our weakness. For we do not
know what to pray for as we ought, but the Spirit himself
intercedes for us with groanings too deep for words. And he who
searches hearts knows what is the mind of the Spirit, because
the Spirit intercedes for the saints according to the will of God.
(Romans 8:26,27)

Whenever we find ourselves stumped in prayer, Jesus
encourages us that the Father always gives the Holy Spirit to
those who ask (Luke 11:9-13).

Jesus' practice of prayer is a pattern for us.

Jesus' life of prayer is outlined in fullness and detail, especially
in the book of Luke, to furnish a clear pattern for how we, like
Jesus, are to navigate life by prayer, enjoy our union with God
through prayer, and call down the kingdom realities of grace and
power using prayer.

I recall the first time I read the many passages about Jesus' prayer life from Luke's gospel. I studied them one at a time and all together. It was not only Jesus' teaching about prayer but his very praying life that overwhelmed me with its simplicity. Jesus said, "Follow me!" If I was going to follow him and become like him, I needed to live a life of prayer like he did. I knew this would disrupt my way of life, but I was sure it would be infinitely worth it.

Studying the prayer practices of Jesus has become both a discipline and a habit for me. Like Jesus praying all night before choosing his disciples, I want to learn to face every significant decision with prayer. Like Jesus, who met exhaustion by withdrawing to desolate places to pray, I am learning to restore and renew by hours and days spent alone with God. Like Jesus, I hope to have a contagious prayer life, which comes from spending much time with him in prayer.

Jesus is the supreme teacher of prayer, and he invites us into his school of prayer. He demonstrates to us what a praying life looks like. He provides models for prayer, and we can overlay his prayer life on ours to cultivate richer prayer lives.

We invite you to read, meditate, and pray through the following Scriptures. Learn what a praying life is about by studying the prayer life of Jesus. One at a time these texts have weight—read together, they will carry you to new heights of joy and adventure in prayer.

As you read, pray. Allow the Word to do the speaking, to teach you what you must learn from Jesus' life of prayer. Overlay Jesus' prayer life onto your own. At first, the contrast might seem overwhelming, yet as you follow his example step by step, you will be inspired to pray and will begin to emulate his life of prayer.

From the start, Jesus lives a life of prayer.

Jesus' baptism inaugurates his ministry. The Spirit falls upon him while he is praying.

6

Now when all the people were baptized, and when Jesus also had been baptized and was praying, the heavens were opened, and the Holy Spirit descended on him in bodily form, like a dove; and a voice came from heaven, "You are my beloved Son; with you I am well pleased." (Luke 3:21,22)

Similarly, the entire Christian life begins with prayer. Martin Luther said, "Prayer is the first breath of a new believer." If that first breath does not happen, life cannot begin. Once the first breath happens, the rest of life is simply a matter of continuing to breathe.

Before Jesus begins his public ministry, he prays, fasts, and fights the devil for forty days: *"Jesus, full of the Holy Spirit, returned from the Jordan and was led by the Spirit in the wilderness for forty days, being tempted by the devil." (Luke 4:1)*

Those who are weak in faith meet adversity with anxiety. Jesus' followers face the enemy with prayer.

Jesus prays to recover from ministry chaos.

We leave our busy lives to pray. Jesus left his praying life to be busy: *"But now, even more, the report about him went abroad, and great crowds gathered to hear him and to be healed of their infirmities. But he would withdraw to desolate places and pray." (Luke 5:15-16)*

Jesus prays in advance of major decisions.

At every critical juncture in life, Jesus turns to prayer: *"In these days he went out to the mountain to pray, and all night he continued in prayer to God. And when day came, he called his disciples and chose from them twelve, whom he named apostles." (Luke 6:12-13)*

For Jesus, prayer initiates every kingdom advance. The author Luke takes pains to present this fact with indisputable detail. How much more should this become true of us? How foolish for us to make our important plans and decisions with little or no prayer! Planning for the future moves us from anxiety and uncertainty to adventure and opportunity when we immerse our decision-making in prayer. As we pray and fast, we partner with Christ, and we learn to yield to the guidance of the Holy Spirit.

Jesus at prayer elicits the first great confession.

Time and again, Jesus retreats to be alone with God, and the disciples notice. Eventually, they figure and out and realize that this man of prayer is the Son of God:

> *Now it happened that as he was praying alone, the disciples were with him. And he asked them, "Who do the crowds say that I am?" And they answered, "John the Baptist. But others say, Elijah, and others, that one of the prophets of old has risen." Then he said to them, "But who do you say that I am?" And Peter answered, "The Christ of God." (Luke 9:18-20)*

Someone once said, "We are what we pray." Jesus' identity is most clearly revealed as he prays. Likewise, our true identity is revealed by our prayer lives. Others cannot fail to notice.

While praying, Jesus is transfigured.

Prayer is the environment of transfiguration:

> *Now about eight days after these sayings he took with him Peter and John and James and went up on the mountain to pray. And as he was praying, the appearance of his face was altered, and his clothing became dazzling white. (Luke 9:28-29)*

It is while he prays that Jesus manifests his glory. It is in earnest prayer that Christ's followers see the vision of his splendor and glory. Apart from our prayers, Christ's glory remains hidden.

Jesus' prayer life inspires his disciples to pray.

Jesus not only prays—his prayer life is contagious: *"Now Jesus was praying in a certain place, and when he finished, one of his disciples said to him, "Lord, teach us to pray, as John taught his disciples." (Luke 11:1ff)*

The disciples have just returned from a mission trip. They preached the gospel, healed the sick, and fought demonic forces. They are excited by their ministry but have awakened to the enormous challenges before them. Prayer has moved them from pious practice to urgent necessity. Hungry for Jesus' power and peace, the disciples turn to the great teacher to learn his secret of kingdom advance.

Too often, believers today hide in the safe confines of the local church. Separated from the harvest field, they feel little hunger for prayer. It is only those who step forth in obedience to the mission who urgently seek out Christ to teach them how to pray.

Jesus cleanses the temple because of prayer.

Jesus is hailed as Messiah as he enters the city. Descending from the Mount of Olives, he surveys Jerusalem and weeps for her. She has no eyes or heart for his coming, and Jesus prophesies terrible judgments on the city and her inhabitants.

> *Your enemies will set up a barricade around you and surround you and hem you in on every side and tear you down to the ground, you and your children within you...because you did not know the time of your visitation."* (Luke 19: 43,44)

The next day, Jesus enters the temple. Eaten up by jealousy for God's honor, his words of judgment become actions of wrath *"And he entered the temple and began to drive out those who sold, saying to them, 'It is written, 'My house shall be a house of prayer,' but you have made it a den of robbers."* (Luke 19:45-46)

At the temple we see Jesus as we have never seen him before. He holds court, pronounces the verdict, and executes the judgment of God. The reason for his fury is straightforward but profound—God intends his temple to be a place for all nations to gather in prayer. All the splendor of this building, the temple service, teaching, and sacrifices mean nothing if prayer for the nations is missing.

9

The same holds true today. The cleansing of the temple is a monumental call to prayer for all time. Building projects, Sunday services, excellent programs, and offerings of money and time mean nothing if we are not building the Father's house of prayer for a lost world.

In anguished prayer, Jesus prepares for the cross

Jesus could not have faced the cross without prayer. He did not set aside his human nature to bear our sin—he faced the cross in his full humanity in order to be our representative. Apart from the power given to him as he cried out in prayer, his approaching murder at the hands of men was more than he could possibly bear: *"And being in agony he prayed more earnestly; and his sweat became like great drops of blood falling down to the ground."* (Luke 22:44)

Jesus was only able to face his greatest challenge by collapsing before his Father in prayer. How much more do we need to face the most significant challenges of life and death by crying out to our Father?

Jesus forgives his enemies on the cross.

The challenge of forgiveness is in proportion to the cost of forgiveness. It is no challenge to forgive a nickel debt—it is a considerable challenge to forgive a million dollars. The highest cost of forgiveness is to forgive someone for taking a life. Jesus paid the highest cost of forgiveness because he paid the highest price: *"And Jesus said, 'Father, forgive them, for they know not what they do.' And they cast lots to divide his garments."* (Luke 23:34)

The greater the injury done to us, the greater the need for us to ask again and again for Christ's Spirit of forgiving prayer. One person put it this way: "Forgiving again?" I asked in dismay. "Must I keep forgiving and forgiving always?" "No," said the angel, whose eye pierced me through, "Stop forgiving when the Savior stops forgiving you."

Jesus surrenders his soul in prayer.

Jesus begins his ministry in prayer, and he ends his ministry in prayer.

It was now about the sixth hour, and there was darkness over the whole land until the ninth hour, while the sun's light failed. And the curtain of the temple was torn in two. Then Jesus, calling out with a loud voice, said, "Father, into your hands I commit my spirit!" And having said this he breathed his last. (Luke 23:44-46)

This cosmic prayer of surrender expresses Christ's final release and paramount accomplishment for humankind. Prayer and surrender are synonymous—all true and effective prayer commits our spirit into the hands of God.

Jesus prays blessing upon his followers at his ascension.

As he ascends to his eternal reign, Jesus lifts his hands to pray: *"And he led them out as far as Bethany, and lifting up his hands he blessed them. While he blessed them, he parted from them and was carried up into heaven."* (Luke 24:50)

His hands are lifted still! He ever lives to pray his resurrection blessings upon his people (Romans 8:34). We are most like the risen and exalted Christ when we bless others in intercession.

The Christian life is many things, but it certainly involves the active imitation of Christ. Imitating others is not wrong. The apostle Paul tells the Corinthian believers, *"Imitate me as I imitate Christ."* (1 Corinthians 11:1).

We can imitate Jesus following the example of godly women and men of prayer—people who "example" a life of prayer. Their contagious integrity draws us into their leadership. We intuit their godliness comes from following Jesus. Their passion for God makes us want to imitate them so that we too can experience and enter the prayer life of Jesus.

Letting older and wiser believers model integrity of life, largeness of faith, and passion for mission reveals what following Jesus looks like. Sheep follow their shepherds. The next generation depends on it!

KINGDOM-COME PRAYER TODAY

1. Evaluate your prayer life in light of Jesus' prayer life. Note where there are differences. Ask God to help you lead and serve "from the knees" as Jesus did.

2. How are you currently handling major decisions or challenges in your life? To what degree are you driven by worry rather than empowered through prayer? What will it take to move from anxiety to adventure?

3. When depleted and exhausted, what do you do? How do you feel about taking a day of restful prayer like Jesus? *"In returning and rest you shall be saved; in quietness and in trust shall be your strength."* (Isaiah 30:15)

CHAPTER 2

The King's Strategy for Prayer

Jesus' Prayer Expands Our Heart for God and His Mission

J esus came to build a new world, and this calls for a new prayer. Not just any prayer will do. He trains his disciples in a prayer that contains the architecture and strategy to advance the kingdom. He gives them a prayer that will increase their capacity for God and expand their heart for others.

Jesus knows we need help to pray—we do not know what to ask for and we do not know how to ask. In order to impart his purposes and his passion for prayer, he gives an all-purpose framework to guide our prayers. Praying the priorities of this prayer is the key to the growth and advance of the kingdom of God. It is the prayer of all prayers; we call it "The Lord's Prayer."

When the disciples approach Jesus and request, "Lord teach us to pray," they have seen Jesus "praying in a certain place." They realize that his peace with God and his power for mission flow from a life of prayer. They are hungry to experience the same peace and power. They are eager to know the secret of effective prayer. Jesus responds to the disciples' request by providing them with a comprehensive framework, a grid for prayer.

A prayer for busy people

We have always been busy—even Jesus was so busy he had to retreat to pray. Today's world is not only busy, it lacks cohesion—fragmented and distracted as it is by digital media and technology. We are devoted to scientific progress, but have no "faith trajectory." We move at break-neck speed, but have no purpose or destiny to chart the course. It is marvelous how the prayer of Jesus speaks to this very need. Using the Lord's Prayer as a framework for prayer is one way of incorporating structure into a busy and fragmented life. (See Appendix B).

During my travels, a busy wife and mother of young children wanted me to know, "As you suggested some years ago, I retained the Lord's prayer as the framework for my praying. It brings order and purpose into my busy and scattered life. I don't know what I would do without it. I have shared it with other mothers of young children, and they use it too."

A prayer to build the kingdom

Our Father in heaven, hallowed be your name.
Your kingdom come, your will be done, on earth as it is in heaven.
Give us this day our daily bread,
And forgive us our debts, as we also have forgiven our debtors.
And lead us not into temptation, but deliver us from evil.

(Matthew 6:9ff)

As you begin to pray this prayer, the words might sound like so many high-sounding phrases. However, as you faithfully persist, two great transformations occur. Praying this prayer increases your capacity for God and expands your heart for others.

First of all, the capacity of your heart for God will dramatically increase. The priority of the Lord's prayer is the Lord, therefore meaningful and effective prayer begins with a focus on God. His fatherhood, holy name, kingdom, and will are the heart and wellspring of this prayer. Worshiping God, seeking his kingdom, and acting on his will raise our prayers from mundane matters to eternal realities.

God is eager to give himself to us. Jesus assures those who pray that God will give them the Holy Spirit: How much more will the heavenly Father give the Holy Spirit to those who ask him! The central answer to our prayer is God. Augustine said it best, "Prayer increases our capacity for God's gift of himself."

Second, your heart will expand until you share Christ's own passion for his church and his sacrificial love for a lost world. Pray this prayer and you will move from uncaring selfishness to wholehearted intercession. God will lift you from the narrow confines of present urgencies to the majestic vision of a world transformed through answered prayer. Your commitment and resolve to build Christ's kingdom will deepen. Slowly but certainly, you will begin to embody the Lord's kingdom values and be compelled to carry out his kingdom directives. As he fills you with the Holy Spirit, you will become the salt of the earth, the light of the world, and the leaven that spreads throughout a lost and needy world.

The direction of our prayers

We become what we pray. When prayer neglects Christ's kingdom priorities, it becomes constricted and suffocates under a burden of present urgencies. Our prayers focus on a random set of personal problems and health-related challenges. This kind of prayer accomplishes little transformation for those who pray and little for the world in which we live. Answers are few and far between.

DEFAULT PRAYER constricts
our capacity for God and others

While in Coimbatore, India, I spent two days with the leaders and staff of Serve India, I came to realize the expansive capacities of the Lord's Prayer with renewed clarity. I was showing these leaders how to use the Lord's Prayer as a grid to bring a kingdom framework and purpose to their prayers. As we were discussing and praying, I came to a liberating realization: not only did praying according to Jesus' "grid" bring a high purpose and kingdom order to my prayer life, but it was also expanding my heart into the greater parameters of the kingdom. Praying the way Jesus taught us to pray was increasing my capacity for God and expanding my heart for others.

Even as I was teaching others, God was speaking to me about my prayers. He revealed a negative tendency—I had been neglecting my habit to pray along with the Lord's Prayer, and the result was that my prayer requests were becoming constricted to personal urgencies and concerns. I was not asking for wrong things, but my prayers were becoming self-focused. God opened my eyes to see that praying through the Lord's Prayer was a powerful way to counter this tendency.

I realized that by neglecting to pray at Jesus taught, I was losing a great deal of the joy and power I previously experienced when using the Lord's Prayer. The contrast was obvious.

Beginning with the first four petitions of the prayer, I would start by meditating on the fatherhood of God, move to reverencing his holy name, progress to enjoying the splendor and majesty of his kingdom, and then yielding to his will. The longer I continue a thoughtful and interactive practice of focusing on God, slowly but surely, my capacity for God was growing.

As I prayed the last three petitions by praying for myself and others, my perspective was changing. The more I prayed for "today's bread," the more I experienced personal contentment and generosity. By repeatedly asking God to forgive my debts, I was enabled both to extend and receive forgiveness. Praying this way was making me a kinder person. As I asked to be delivered from temptation and to be guided by God's Spirit, I was placing myself, and others under the protection of God. In the process, my experience of God's leading moved from theory to reality.

Praying the way Jesus prayed was setting me free from constricted prayer, opening my heart to receive God's gift of himself, and reversing my selfish tendencies.

As it turns out, God was communicating a similar message to the Indian pastors and leaders. At lunch, a young man, alight with passionate energy, asked if I would capture his prayer testimonial on video. He was eager to share his joy with people in North Amercia. Here are some of his own words:

> This has been a divine revelation. My fingers were tingling as you spoke. I could feel that I was being filled with the Spirit when you taught us how to pray the Lord's Prayer. Many people in India believe that if they simply say the words of this prayer, they are Christians. This is a very great error. You have been teaching us that if we pray this way, we will be praying for great and important things.

In contrast to default prayer, "the Lord's prayer" is the prayer Jesus gives his people. This is the prayer Jesus prayed, and the Father always hears the Son (John 11:41). As God answers these seven petitions, the aims, values and goals of Christ's kingdom enter the fabric and heart of our lives. The Lord's prayer increases our capacity for God and expands our heart for others.

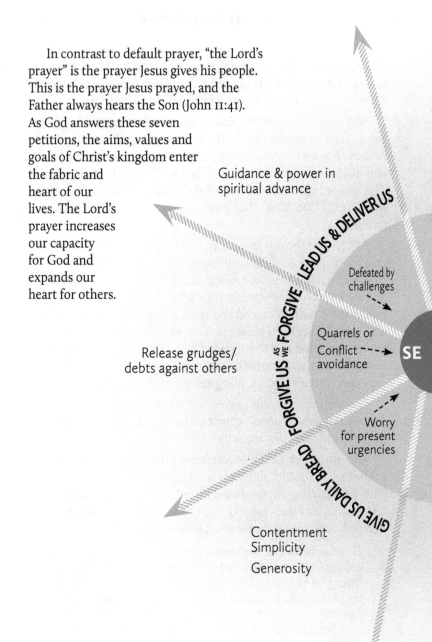

Guidance & power in spiritual advance

LEAD US & DELIVER US

Defeated by challenges

FORGIVE US AS WE FORGIVE

Quarrels or Conflict avoidance

SE

Release grudges/ debts against others

Worry for present urgencies

GIVE US DAILY BREAD

Contentment
Simplicity
Generosity

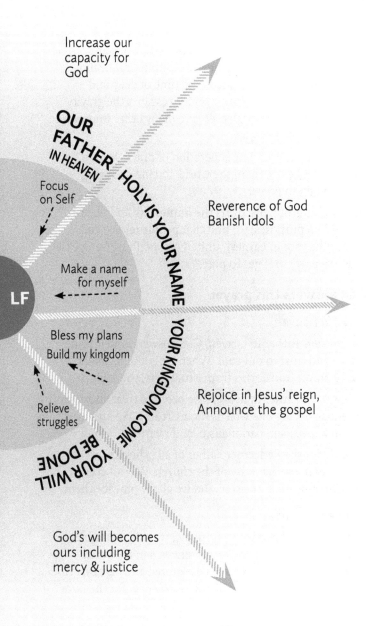

Increase our
capacity for
God

OUR
FATHER
IN HEAVEN

HOLY IS YOUR NAME

Focus
on Self

Reverence of God
Banish idols

Make a name
for myself

LF

Bless my plans
Build my kingdom

YOUR KINGDOM COME

Relieve
struggles

Rejoice in Jesus' reign,
Announce the gospel

BE DONE
YOUR WILL

God's will becomes
ours including
mercy & justice

As our prayers constrict, they tend to be sparse on praise and focused on limited requests. At various studies and meetings, invariably the time comes for prayer requests. For some unknown reason, most requests start with a narrative of someone's health crisis and the request is for physical healing. We seldom begin our prayers with a long time of deep and meaningful worship of God. Prayer seldom escapes the gravity of our small world, even though there are many other important things we should be praying for.

If we hope to raise up a new generation of prayer leaders, we will need to set before them the world and life-changing mandates of kingdom prayer.

When a prayer group discovers the immensity and majesty of God's kingdom purposes, we find that people rejoice and begin to raise the roof in earnest, united prayer. Prayer moves from "I have to pray" to "I get to pray."

How God answers this prayer

Our Father in heaven

As we pray Our Father in heaven, God answers, and it brings childlike love and trust to our soul. When we address God as Father, every prayer transforms from ritual to relationship.

As we pray Our Father in heaven, we begin to treat all people as created equal, having one God as their Creator. We are praying against tribalism, nationalism, and racism.

Because God is the Redeemer Father of all believers, we become passionate for the unity of the church. We call every believer in Christ brother or sister, and we gladly pray for them.

Hallowed be your name

When we pray Hallowed be your name, we gain a humble sense of awe at God's holiness. We are renewed in reverence and become jealous for his name to be honored and his fame to spread throughout the world (Isaiah 66:9). We pray for the pure worship of God in his church. With this fuller vision of God, we experience new depths of repentance and new fillings of joy.

When we ask Hallowed be your name, we grieve when men misuse or dishonor his name or fail to give him thanks. We focus our resolve on proclaiming the fame and glory of God to those who do not know him (Psalm 96). We anticipate a day when all mankind will be a multi-national, multi-billion voice choir!

Your kingdom come

As we call out from the heart Your kingdom, come, we rejoice in Christ's rule and reign, and we are captured by the majesty of his mission. As we go deep in prayer, Jesus gives us his heart for those who do not know him. When he saw the crowds, he had compassion for them, because they were harassed and helpless, like sheep without a shepherd (Matthew 9:36). Our prayers are filled with zeal for his mission: *"The harvest is plentiful, but the laborers are few; therefore pray earnestly to the Lord of the harvest."* (Matthew 9:37-38)

As we pray, we move from being spectators to becoming participants in his mission: *"As you sent me into the world, so I have sent them into the world."* (John 17:18) Jesus said, *"The Son of Man came to seek and save the lost."* (Luke 19:10) As we pray, his purpose becomes ours: many people come to Christ and revival in the church and renewal for the city follow (see Zechariah 13:1,2).

Your will be done on earth as it is in heaven

When we pray Your will be done on earth as it is in heaven, a miracle happens within. God's will moves into our hearts. From within, we strive to accept his will, no matter how difficult things get. We learn to approve God's will as good and right and just; we resolve to act on his will in loving obedience.

As we faithfully pray Your will be done on earth as it is in heaven, we feel our souls burn with God's love of righteousness and justice: *"What does the Lord require of you but to do justice and to love kindness and walk humbly with your God?"* (Micah 6:8)We move from being overwhelmed by the injustice of the world to becoming agents of its renewal. Our kingdom prayers bring justice and mercy to realization. We become God's answer to our own prayers.

> *Then you shall call, and the Lord will answer; you shall cry, and he will say, "Here I am"… If you pour yourself out for the hungry and satisfy the desire of the afflicted…you shall raise up the foundations of many generations; you shall be called the repairer of the breach, the restorer of streets to dwell in.* (Isaiah 58:9-12)

Give us this day our daily bread

As we request of God to Give us this day our daily bread, we trust in firm assurance that we will have enough resources for ourselves and plenty to care for the poor and needy. Our hearts become generous, and our needs modest. We are filled with a new spirit of thanksgiving.

As we pray Give us today our daily bread, we learn contentment and generosity. We don't just talk about helping others in need—we start doing it, giving our time and releasing our resources and opening our homes to the poor, displaced, disabled, immigrant, or otherwise outcast.

Forgive us our debts as we forgive our debtors

When we humbly pray Forgive us our debts as we forgive our debtors, we are asking God to impart his Spirit and grant redemptive community. God gives us a deep inner peace as we accept and enjoy his forgiveness. Whether in the church or in the world, we begin to treat others with humility and grace.

As we bow in humble repentance, asking God to Forgive our debts, he makes us agents of reconciliation. An elderly friend knew her cancer was a death sentence. She shared with me, "I was praying 'Forgive us our debts,' and all of a sudden, I knew my heart was filled with grudges toward family members. I realized how foolish I was. I phoned each of them to say 'I am sorry.' They forgave me. Now they are all coming here for a family reunion." As she conveyed this story, her eyes radiated pure joy.

Lead us not into temptation but deliver us from the evil one

When we pray Lead us not into temptation, God fortifies our soul against the incessant temptations of the world and the devil. Guided by the Good Shepherd, we grow confident that he will lead us in the way we should go. We pray to be led by Jesus and to be kept in his "paths of righteousness for his name's sake" (Psalm 23:3). By definition, sheep that do not follow the shepherd get lost and find themselves in trouble. Lose sight of Jesus and we will certainly fall into temptation and evil.

When we pray this petition, we are like Frodo Baggins when he put on the ring of power. That very instant he was in full view of unseen realities. He was able to discern the enemy— and the enemy was able to see him. We do not pray about spiritual warfare. Prayer itself is spiritual warfare. We are not overwhelmed or fearful because Jesus came to destroy the works of the devil (1 John 3:8), and indeed he did. At the cross, he dealt the death-blow to the evil one.

Praying "Lead us not into temptation" makes us aware of the evil, dark pride, licentious, and anti-Christian nature of the world around us—and the world within us, too. We join others praying against the predatory and immoral actions of those who deceive others, who use all manner of schemes to exploit people, from dishonest marketing to human trafficking. We cultivate godliness and encourage strong boundaries around our churches, families, and communities. We endeavor to use "just weights" and honest communications in all our dealings.

Answers to prayer depend what we ask for. Jesus taught, "Ask and you shall receive." When we pray using Jesus' guide to prayer, God's first answer is the gift of himself. As we pray, he increases our capacity for the gift of himself and expands our hearts with a growing love for others. Within these two rich blessings come the specific answers to our requests.

Renee Reynolds is a prayer director for Geneva School in New York City. She has been using the Lord's Prayer as a grid and framework for her prayers for years. Renee reflects:

Using the seven-day prayer outline has fortified my prayer life with structure, dimension, and meaning—but most of all, with a God-aligned focus and God-glorifying intent. I find the grid a simple tool that can be adapted to suit a diversity of people and personalities. Noting answered prayers fosters ongoing gratitude and reinvigorated prayer. (note: see Appendix B)

What Jesus' prayer accomplishes

Jesus creates a new world order—and he gives a prayer to accomplish that end. Praying these seven petitions on your own and in community will forever deliver you from constricted and self-focused prayer. It will introduce you to—and invite you into— the advance of God's kingdom.

Our Lord aims to transform us into his likeness. He honors us by enlisting us in his world-changing mission. In order to expand our hearts and accomplish his kingdom purposes, he teaches us to pray the directives of this supreme "kingdom-come" prayer. Hear the words of Tertullian, who contrasts prayer before the coming of Christ and after his coming, highlighting what mighty things prayer can now do:

Of old, prayer was able to rescue from fire and beasts and hunger, even before it received its perfection from Christ. How much greater then is the power of Christian prayer. No longer does prayer bring an angel of comfort to the heart of a fiery furnace, or close up the mouths of lions, or transport to the hungry food from the fields. No longer does it remove all sense of pain by the grace it wins for others. But it gives the armour of patience to those who suffer, who feel pain, who are distressed. It strengthens the power of grace, so that faith may know what is gaining from the Lord, and understand what it is suffering for the name of God.

In the past prayer was able to bring down punishment, rout armies, withhold the blessing of rain. Now, however, the prayer of the just turns aside the whole anger of God, keeps vigil for its enemies, pleads for persecutors. Prayer is the one thing that can conquer God. But Christ has willed that it should work no evil, and has given it all power over good. Its only art is to call back the souls of the dead from the very journey into death, to give strength to the weak, to heal the sick, to exorcise the possessed, to open prison cells, to free the innocent from their chains. Prayer cleanses from sin, drives away temptations, stamps out persecutions, comforts the fainthearted, gives new strength to the courageous, brings travelers safely home, calms the waves, confounds robbers, feeds the poor, overrules the rich, lifts up the fallen, supports those who are falling, sustains those who stand firm.

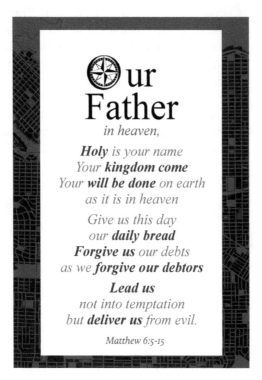

✸ur
Father
in heaven,

Holy *is your name*
Your **kingdom come**
Your **will be done** *on earth*
as it is in heaven

Give us this day
our **daily bread**
Forgive us *our debts*
as we **forgive our debtors**

Lead us
not into temptation
but **deliver us** *from evil.*

Matthew 6:5-15

KINGDOM-COME PRAYER TODAY

1. Evaluate the health of your current prayer life. Review the seven priorities of the Lord's Prayer. Choose one petition and compare it with your present prayer life.

2. Are you praying in the way Jesus taught us to pray? Don't just think it over. Pray it through with Jesus. Let him be your prayer teacher as he was with his twelve disciples.

3. Pray for the church to be revived. Pray for the gospel to reach a lost world, specifically your lost city or town. Pray for many to enter the kingdom by faith. Pray for the city's flourishing and renewal.

4. For a practical 7 day framework to guide your daily prayers to the priorites in the Lord's prayer, please see Appendix B.

CHAPTER 3

The King's Passion for Kingdom Prayer

When Jesus Visits His People, He Draws a Line in the Sand

The coming of the King overthrows the existing order. Consider the turmoil when Jesus comes to the temple in Jerusalem.

It's Palm Sunday. Early in the day Jesus descends from the Mount of Olives, and all heaven breaks loose. Disciples and children crowd the gates and surround the city with loud hosannas. When commanded to stop their singing, Jesus says, *"I tell you, if these were silent, the very stones would cry out."* (Luke 19:40)

Then, as the crowd comes over the crest of the mountain, Jerusalem comes into full view, and the procession halts.

Overlooking Jerusalem, Jesus weeps for the city and prophesies her destruction. Everything seems in good order, but one thing is missing—the rulers and people of the city have failed to recognize the coming of their king. *"Therefore, they will not leave one stone upon another in you (Jerusalem), because you did not know the time of your visitation."* (Luke 19:44)

The procession passes through the Kidron Valley and up toward the city walls. While the children continue their loud singing, Jesus enters and surveys the temple.

Viewed from the outside, things seem to be running smoothly. Herod's glorious structure rivals Solomon's temple, daily sacrifices are being offered, priests and Levites are consecrated to the liturgy and service. Yet, one essential thing is missing. The temple is not a house of prayer for the nations.

God's passion for the nations

In order that the entire world might hear of God's fame and declare his glory, God had his people build a temple to be the place of his "holy habitation." His intent was to provide a welcoming place for foreigners from every nation to stream in, learn about the one true God, and pray to him.

> *And the foreigners who join themselves to the Lord, to minister to him, to love the name of the Lord and to be his servants, everyone who keeps the Sabbath and does not profane it, and holds fast my covenant—these I will bring to my holy mountain, and make them joyful in my house of prayer; for my house shall be called a house of prayer for all peoples.* (Isaiah 56:6-7)

God's passion for his own glory and his vision for a worldwide church come together in this vision of a house of prayer. The temple must be a house of prayer for the nations or it will miss out on Gods purpose. The temple must have open gates or it will not fulfill God's vision.

God's passion for the nations is found throughout the Scriptures. For example, Isaiah pictures a day when all peoples will join in praying and worshiping God. Those who have been rescued by God will announce his royal splendor and gather the nations into his temple:

> *I will send some of those who survive to the nations... and to the distant islands that have not heard of my fame or seen my glory. They will proclaim my glory among the nations. And they will bring all your people, from all the nations, to my holy mountain in Jerusalem as an offering to the Lord. From one New Moon to another and from one Sabbath to another, all mankind will come and bow down before me....* (Isaiah 66:19-23)

A missed opportunity

At different times in church history there have been great opportunities to declare God's glory among the nations. One of the greatest, with the saddest outcome, happened during the reign of the mighty Kublai Khan. In 1271 Kublai established the Yuan dynasty, which ruled over present-day Mongolia, China, and Korea. By 1279 the Mongol conquest of the Song dynasty was completed and Kublai became the first non-native emperor to conquer all of China.

Kublai Khan did not hate Christians—in fact, he had great respect for them. He was curious about Christian kings and princes and wanted to know more about the Pope and how Christians worshiped. When Niccolò and Maffeo Polo, Marco Polo's father and uncle, were returning to Venice after their first visit, the Khan sent a letter to the Pope with them. It was a challenge. He wanted the Pope to send a hundred missionaries prepared to proselytize. These missionaries would be given opportunity to show that the Christian faith was superior to others. If the Khan could be convinced, he was ready to become a man of the Church (without, however, renouncing the Mongolian religion). The Polos gave Khan's letter to the newly elected Pope, and yet Gregory X could spare only two Dominican monks instead of the hundred. Here was a great opportunity to change the course of history—and the people of God missed it.

Jesus as we have never seen him before

Palm Sunday is no ordinary day and this is no ordinary visit to the temple. This is Jesus' day of reckoning. He will measure the temple practices by the yardstick of sincere prayers and hospitality.

Jesus enters Jerusalem and surveys the activity at the temple, the temple practices and the conduct of the priests and religious leaders. It is Passover and God's people, the Jews, have gathered from all over the world to keep the feast and remember their momentous deliverance from Egypt. This is a great opportunity to gather those who do not know about God's fame and glory. Jesus expects to see temple doors wide open and the whole city thronging with foreigners who have heard of God's fame and who have come to pray.

He finds just the opposite.

Instead of open doors, the temple gates are crowded with commerce. Foreigners are hindered entrance by the chaotic mercenary proceedings—those who have erected merchant kiosks at the temple entrances to offer foreign-exchange money-changing services and to sell livestock to visitors for their temple sacrifices. If foreigners and visitors manage to navigate this temple-entry chaos, what they find, instead of an inviting place to pray, is a designated fenced-off court far removed from the temple's worship center that has been reserved for Jews. Rather than welcoming the nations, according to the tradition of the elders, Gentile worshipers are treated as unclean. Jewish worshipers are prohibited from touching or even talking with foreigners lest they become unclean (see Acts 10:27-28).

Foreigners are made to feel like customers rather than guests. They are treated as commodities rather than worshipers.

What Jesus surveys is a far cry from God's intended "joyful house of prayer." Foreigners are excluded and prayer has been replaced by commerce. Jesus is furious, literally "eaten up" with jealousy for God (John 2:16-17). *"And he entered the temple and began to drive out those who sold, saying to them, 'It is written, 'My house shall be a house of prayer,' but you have made it a den of robbers."* (Luke 19:45-46)

This is Jesus like we have never seen him! This is Jesus as judge. Righteous anger has been building up in his spirit—it has to erupt. No longer weeping, Jesus comes by storm—he looses the judgment of God upon those who have corrupted the temple courts and burdened would-be worshipers. In John's account we read: *"Making a whip of cords, he drove them all out of the temple, with the sheep and oxen. And he poured out the coins of the money-changers and overturned their tables."* (John 2:16)

This temple cleansing hearkens back to the temple cleansings by the revival-era kings in the monarchy of Judah. We see this jealous fury in Nehemiah: *"And I was very angry and I threw all the household furniture of Tobiah out of the chamber. Then I gave orders, and they cleansed the chambers...."* (Nehemiah 13:8-9)

Jesus' cleansing of the temple fulfills Malachi's prophesy of the ultimate visitation and purifying of the temple by the "messenger of the covenant":

> *Behold, I send my messenger, and he will prepare the way before me. And the Lord whom you seek will suddenly come to his temple; and the messenger of the covenant in whom you delight, behold, he is coming, says the Lord of hosts. But who can endure the day of his coming, and who can stand when he appears? For he is like a refiner's fire and like fullers' soap.* (Malachi 3:1-2)

Jesus scatters the purveyors of greed. He is the refiner's fire, purifying his people in cleansing, white-hot anger. On this day, Jesus draws a line in the sand—from now on insiders will be left out and outsiders brought in. Unlike other revivals, after this cleansing there will be no repentance and no return to the old ways. Christ, as Lord and Judge, has given the verdict and pronounced the final judgment. The people of God have been weighed and found wanting; the kingdom will be taken from them. The old temple will be reduced to ruins, and a new temple, made of living stones, will rise from the rubble.

Christ's reckoning is based on a single factor—he measures and weighs his temple by the measure of prayer. Above all and before all, God's house must be a house of prayer for all nations.

Application to our time

I have returned many times to ponder this watershed event. One day it dawned on me to ask, "Is Jesus still drawing the same line in the sand today?" Jesus' words and actions are clear. On that day, he measured the church, "Build my house of prayer. If you fail to do this, you forfeit your role in the advance of the Kingdom." It seemed inescapable logic—if it was true for the church of that day, it must be true for the church today. The line in the sand remains. Jesus is still telling his church to build a house of prayer. He is still calling, "Open our doors to the nations and build my house of prayer. As you do, you will be fulfilling your Father's purpose and promise."

This is not a theoretical issue. The urgency of Jesus' words and actions compel me every time I think of them. Too often, we are afflicted with the same malady Jesus encountered at the temple—prayerlessness and indifference to the fate of those outside. To give the matter more immediacy we can ask, "If Jesus were to turn up in our churches today, would he find that we are building his house of prayer? Would he commend our efforts or would he bring out the whip and overturn the tables of our commerce and busyness?"

One day soon Jesus will return and visit his people, and he will draw a line in the sand. Even now our risen King weighs the works of the churches. With eyes ablaze, he searches hearts and minds to find if his people remain true to him with all their hearts (Revelation 2:18 ff).

From the events at the temple on Palm Sunday, we learn that the call to earnest united prayer is not just a good idea or a mere sidebar highlighting a biblical priority. Becoming a house of prayer for the nations is at the very heart of the kingdom because it is at the very heart of our King. As leaders and people, we must continually build Jesus' house of prayer. We must pray passionately and persistently for the nations to hear of God's fame. Christ draws the line. Woe to us if we fail to take heed!

How to get started building Jesus' house of prayer

To become Jesus' house of prayer, we must first of all examine our hearts. Then we must review our present practices through the prism of prayer.

Prayer goes to the heart of the matter

For heart transformation to occur, we need to take time to fast and pray. Until we have a holy resolve given by Christ's Spirit, there will be no progress. As we pray, we behold the glory of God (2 Corinthians 3:16-18). As we pray, Jesus' zeal for God's fame is internalized. As we pray, our affections pivot to the glory of God, a love for the nations, and a passion for prayer.

Zeal for God comes first. Jesus loved his creation, but he was not a humanitarian. Jesus' actions were not motivated by the interests of man but rather driven by a passion for God's glory (cf. Matthew 16:23). Yet, the more we are jealous for God, the more we will be moved to reach and serve a lost world. Zeal for God's name is the wellspring of passion for a lost world. Prayer increases our capacity for God and, at the same time, expands our heart for others.

Pray about prayer

We need to weigh our present practices by Christ's standard. We need to ask some important questions; "Are we seeking, through our church communities, to build a house of prayer for the nations?" and "If prayer is not first, then what is?" If prayer is missing, then we must ask, "What has replaced prayer?" This means examining our motives as well as our actions. In what ways have we made attendance data and financial metrics higher priorities than prayer and hospitality? In what ways have we blocked the gates to would-be worshipers?

For prayer to permeate all we do, we first need to search out and replace any prayer-less meetings and self-directed planning sessions.

Each wrong motive and practice that has replaced prayer needs to be confessed. Prayer must be restored to its rightful place. As we repent, God forgives us, he renews our spirits, and prayer becomes central to all of ministry, mission, and life.

Becoming a praying church or praying mission is not something that happens automatically. Just as we need training and discipleship in studying the Word, we equally need to be trained in prayer. Few education programs in church, school, Bible school, seminary, or mission training include prayer training. We have even lost prayer in our homes. Much repenting and rebuilding will need to happen for God's people to become a house of prayer.

Again, and again, we must ask where have doors been closed to would-be God worshipers. Has our church or mission become ingrown?

Thousands of people from hundreds of nations, including new immigrants, refugees, and international students, are streaming into our cities, presenting tremendous opportunities for us to introduce them to Christ. In our experience, we have found that hosting them in homes, inviting them to fellowship activities, taking them on outings, bringing them to church, and introducing them to Christian music have all been received with great joy. Yet, for example in Canada, over 90 percent of international students never get invited into a Canadian home. Immigrants and refugees are scared and confused and long for a welcoming word and any type of personal kindness.

Prayer groups for missions here and abroad are essential for building a house of prayer for the nations. Pray for international students who are so often receptive to the gospel. Pray for the persecuted church and you will also be praying for a mighty advance of the kingdom.[1] Pray for the Muslim world, where God is doing a great work of salvation.[2]

An Example from History:
THE MORAVIAN AWAKENING (1727)

One of the most long-lasting prayer and mission movements began with the Moravian Awakening in 1727 and continued for 100 years. Count Nicholas von Zinzendorf had gathered diverse religious refugees from surrounding countries, but during its first five years of existence the Herrnhut settlement showed few signs of spiritual power.

In early 1727 the disgruntled community at Herrnhut was deeply divided and critical of one another. Heated controversies threatened to disrupt the community. The majority were from the ancient Moravian Church of the Brethren; other believers attracted to Herrnhut included Lutherans, Reformed, and Anabaptists. They argued about predestination, holiness, and baptism. Zinzendorf visited all the adult members of the deeply divided community, and he drew up a covenant calling upon them to emphasize their agreements rather than stressing their differences.

On May 12, 1727, they all signed an agreement to dedicate their lives, as he dedicated his, to the service of the Lord Jesus Christ.

---

1 *Voice of the Martyrs* is a great resource to aid our prayers in this regard.

2 *Thirty Days of Prayer for the Muslim World* during Ramadan is a way to join millions of Christians. *Perspectives on World Mission,* or the *Kairos* course, can help any believer to become a "World Christian."

On July 22, many of the community covenanted together of their own accord to meet often to pour out their hearts in prayer and hymns.

On August 5, the Count spent the whole night in prayer with a dozen others, following a large midnight meeting for prayer where great emotion had prevailed.

On Wednesday, August 13, the Holy Spirit was poured out on them all. Their prayers were answered in ways far beyond anyone's expectations. Many of them decided to set aside certain times for continued earnest prayer.

Heart-piercing repentance signaled the beginning of this mighty work of God. No one present could tell exactly what happened to the Moravians on Wednesday morning, August 13, 1727 at the specially called Communion service:

> Zinzendorf described it as a "sense of the nearness of Christ." They had stopped judging each other because they had become convinced, each one, of his lack of worth in the sight of God and each felt at this communion to be in view of the noble countenance of the savior. Zinzendorf was overwhelmed with a vision of Jesus love; "O head full of bruises. So full of pain and scorn. In this view of the man of sorrows and acquainted with grief, their hearts told them that He would be their patron and their priest who was at once changing their hearts into oil of gladness and their misery into happiness."

A spirit of prayer was immediately evident in the fellowship and continued throughout that "golden summer of 1727," as the Moravians came to designate the period. On August 27 of that year twenty-four men and twenty-four women covenanted to spend one hour each day in scheduled prayer. Some others en listed in the "hourly intercession." Unbidden, even children gathered in the church to pray.

For over a hundred years, the members of the Moravian Church all shared in the "hourly intercession." At home and abroad, on land and sea, this prayer watch ascended unceasingly to the Lord.

In prayer and the Spirit, the Moravians sent out missionaries and thus news of the revival spread to surrounding nations. Over the next twenty-five years, from that little village one hundred missionaries were sent to the most difficult and destitute regions of the world to preach Christ.

Evan Wiggs. *Moravian Revival.* (Vancouver, WA: Measure of Gold Revival Ministries, 2003). http://www.evanwiggs.com/revival/history/moravian.html)

KINGDOM-COME PRAYER TODAY

1. If you are a believer, you are a temple of God. Where would you place yourself on the spectrum:

A den of thieves  Becoming a house of prayer

If you are a church leader, evaluate your church or mission in the same way.

A den of thieves  Becoming a house of prayer

2. On your own: Take some time to fast and pray with Jesus. Ask him to guide you in becoming "a dwelling (house of prayer) in which God lives by his Spirit." (Ephesians 2:21)

Write two or three practices to move you forward.

3. Get together with others: Pray and discuss: "How can we begin to become a house of prayer?"

Kingdom Prayer
Breaks Out

CHAPTER 4

How Christ's Ascension Brings a New Day for Prayer

We Pray in Union with the Exalted Christ

A s Jesus ascends to heaven, he issues a call to prayer and a promise of power (Acts 1:4,8). As commanded by Jesus, his disciples pray and wait for his promised Spirit. All of a sudden, gale force winds blow. Flames spread through a crowd. Earthquakes shake foundations. The power manifest at Pentecost signals a new day for the world and a new day for prayer.

As we read the narrative of the early church, overwhelming evidence reveals that prayer has been transformed. The volume of answered prayer escalates from intermittent stream to cascading waterfall. In Old Testament history, God periodically and occasionally reveals his presence in miracles. After the ascension, great works of God burst forth with expressive fullness, like flower blossoms in springtime. Winter is long gone. Timid people become courageous as lions, shouting long-kept secrets of heaven from the housetops. Answered prayer moves from rare exception to abiding reality.

Christian prayer is distinguished by answers. In this new day of prayer, we are encouraged to ask away! *"Everyone who asks receives. The one who seeks will find. To the one who knocks it will be opened"* (Luke 11:9-13). Jesus repeats the promise again and again, *"If you ask me anything in my name I will do it!"* (John 14:13-14; 15:6-7; 16:26)

God has always been a prayer-answering God. In countless promises and innumerable events, the Old Testament assures every believer that God hears the prayers of his beloved children. The psalmist celebrates, *"O thou who hearest prayer, to thee shall all flesh come"* (Psalm 65:2) and, *"I love the Lord because he has heard my voice and supplications."* (Psalm 116:1)

Yet, following Christ's resurrection, prayer offered in Jesus' name takes asking and receiving into unlimited realms. Now that salvation has been won at the cross and Jesus is seated in royal power and glory, it might be argued that the chief purpose of prayer is that God answers and gives what we ask for.

For example, in the gospel of John, Jesus foreshadows the coming day of answered prayer; no less than six times he proclaims unbounded promises for those who pray:

> *Truly, truly, I say to you, whoever believes in me will also do the works that I do; and greater works than these will he do, because I am going to the Father. Whatever you ask in my name, this I will do, that the Father may be glorified in the Son.* (John 14:12,13)

> *If you ask me anything in my name, I will do it.* (John 14:14)

> *If you abide in me, and my words abide in you, ask whatever you wish, and it will be done for you. By this my Father is glorified, that you bear much fruit and so prove to be my disciples.* (John 15:7,8)

You did not choose me, but I chose you and appointed you that you should go and bear fruit and that your fruit should abide, so that whatever you ask the Father in my name, he may give it to you. (John 15: 15ff)

I will see you again, and your hearts will rejoice, and no one will take your joy from you. In that day you will ask nothing of me. Truly, truly, I say to you, whatever you ask of the Father in my name, he will give it to you. Until now you have asked nothing in my name. Ask, and you will receive, that your joy may be full. (John 16:23-24)

In that day you will ask in my name, and I do not say to you that I will ask the Father on your behalf; for the Father himself loves you, because you have loved me and have believed that I came from God. (John 16:26-27)

Jesus assigns no limits to answered prayer, only guidelines. For example, we are promised answers to our prayers as we ask in Jesus' name, as we ask for the Father to be glorified, as we abide in Jesus, and as we keep his commandments. The environment of answered prayer is redemptive, not transactional.

Our kingdom prayer focuses on the exalted King.

Christian prayer is radically distinct from all other prayer. When a Christian prays, he has an exalted King ever in mind. Christian prayer rejoices in Christ's ascension and participates in Christ's authority over heaven and earth.

Sometimes we forget to whom we are praying. Attend prayer meetings or listen to Sunday morning prayers, and you might imagine Jesus as a heavenly housekeeper cleaning up mankind's problems, keeping the world tidy and running smoothly. This kind of prayer flows from the mind of man and not from the throne of Christ.

Men and women of prayer do not derive their prayer requests from watching the news, for the world cares little for the purposes of God. Kingdom advance, the essence of history, is edited out. Rather, they get their prayer agenda from studying Scripture and gazing at a risen Savior.

I find when I immerse myself in the teaching of Christ's ascension there are wonderful consequences. The more time I spend studying the ascension and its relation to prayer, the more I realize how pervasive and powerful this teaching is. The New Testament is incandescent with this reality. Up to this point, I had been selling my heart short and missing out on what is perhaps the chief joy and power of prayer. Blinkered, I was unable to fully grasp the magnificent promises flowing from the throne of our exalted Lord.

Waking to this reality, I now eagerly search and study the many passages related to Christ's ascension. Filling my morning devotions with new light and joy are songs that celebrate the ascension, mighty hymns like *Rejoice the Lord is King, All Hail the Power of Jesus Name,* and *Crown Him with Many Crowns.*

Our prayers share in the present rule and reign of Jesus.

At present and forevermore, Jesus sits in triumph on heaven's throne. He is the sole and absolute ruler of heaven and earth. We can remember Jesus on the cross, but it is wrong to imagine him still hanging there. At his resurrection, Jesus tells Mary not to linger at the tomb but to go and tell the others that he has risen and is soon ascending to the Father (John 20:21). To picture Jesus as he is today, envision him as the risen Ruler, seated on a glorious throne with all heaven and earth at his feet, *"far above all rule and authority and power and dominion, and above every name that is named, not only in this age but also in the one to come."* (Ephesians 1:20-21)

As we pray, our eyes of faith are fixed on Christ as he exists now, in unimaginable splendor and blinding glory:

> *His eyes were like a flame of fire, his feet were like burnished bronze, refined in a furnace, and his voice was like the roar of many waters… from his mouth came a sharp two-edged sword, and his face was like the sun shining in full strength.* (Revelation 1:12-18)

Our prayers bring ascension realities into the world.

The Scriptures are shameless in references to the present power of Christ in the life and prayers of a believer. The apostle Paul prays that God fill his people with a consciousness of his resurrection power and Christ's ascension authority:

> *May the God of our Lord Jesus Christ, the Father of glory, give you the Spirit of wisdom and of revelation...that you may know...what is the immeasurable greatness of his power toward us who believe, according to the working of his great might that he worked in Christ when he raised him from the dead and seated him at his right hand in the heavenly places, far above all rule and authority and power and dominion.* (Ephesians 1:17-21)

Ascension prayer is a matter of experiencing Christ's power. Domestic prayers for the status quo betray an emaciated view of Jesus and his coming kingdom; when we "under-conceive" Jesus, we miss out on the power of his triumphant ascension.

Praying into Jesus' power and authority is more than an exercise of our imagination. As we pray, we are supernaturally united with him, and seated with him in heavenly places (Ephesians 2:6). His power is "toward us" and "within us" (Ephesians 1:19, 3:20). What fuels our every prayer is our supernatural union with him: *"And you have been filled in him, who is the head of all rule and authority."* (Colossians 2:9)

When prayer becomes boring and self-centered, it is because we are looking at ourselves and have forgotten to fix our eyes on Jesus. Once we recall that we are united to him in his present power and glory, we become what we pray. Pray to the King, and we become like the King.

You can tell when you are praying in the presence and power of the living Christ. As you contemplate the many facets of Christ's present majesty, your prayers will spontaneously burst into praise: *"Worthy is the Lamb who was slain, to receive power and wealth and wisdom and might and honor and glory and blessing!"* (Revelations 5:11-12) Joyous days of effective ministry begin with full-throated, unrestrained praise of our Redeemer King.

Our prayers recognize Christ's rule over the nations.

Christ declares, *"All authority in heaven and earth has been given to me."* (Matthew 28:18) Christ rules over the rulers of the earth. As we read in Psalm 2:9 and Revelation, Jesus governs the nations with a rod of iron (Revelation 2:27 and 19:15). Like a mighty charioteer who restrains and guides his battle horses with bit and bridle, Christ steers the nations to his desired destiny. The outcome is fixed and certain: the coming day in which every knee will bow in worship to the true, ascended King.

In light of Christ's present rule over the nations, we never merely pray for world peace. Jesus said, *"I have not come to bring peace"* (Matthew 10:34). We are commanded to pray for kings and rulers, that they might submit to his rule and carry out his saving purposes. We do not pray for order in the world—we pray for a new world order.

> *First of all, I urge that prayers and intercessions be made for all men, for kings and all who are in high positions, that we may lead a peaceful and quiet life...This is good in the sight of God our Savior, who desires all men to be saved and come to a knowledge of the truth.* (1 Timothy 2:1-4)

Our prayers partner with Jesus when we pray for justice.

We also pray into the present reign of Christ when we intercede and work for justice and righteousness in our land. At present and until the day he returns, Jesus is executing justice and bringing liberty throughout the world.

> *I have put my Spirit upon him; he will bring forth justice to the nations. He will not cry aloud or lift up his voice, or make it heard in the street; a bruised reed he will not break, and a faintly burning wick he will not quench; he will faithfully bring forth justice. He will not grow faint or be discouraged till he has established justice in the earth; and the coastlands wait for his law.* (Isaiah 42:1-4)

When they pray and work for justice, Christians align themselves with the present rule and reign of Jesus. God hears our prayers for the oppressed and authorizes us to carry out the rebuilding of the city from the ground up.

Then you shall call, and the Lord will answer; you shall cry, and he will say, "Here I am." If you pour yourself out for the hungry and satisfy the desire of the afflicted, the Lord will guide you continually and your ancient ruins shall be rebuilt; you shall raise up the foundations of many generations; you shall be called the repairer of the breach, the restorer of streets to dwell in. (Isaiah 58:7-12)

Jesus does not cry out or lift his voice, but his people do—in prayer! Consider the work of the International Justice Mission, whose mission is captured by their motto: "The work of justice begins with prayer." These bold Christians raise a cry to God before they lift up their voice to defend the captive, enslaved, trafficked and oppressed of the world. Daily morning prayer, regular days of prayer, as well as an annual two-day Global Prayer Conference, has fueled their passion for justice.

Our prayers anticipate the return of the King.

The long-awaited King is coming soon, and what a coming it will be!

For as the lightning comes from the east and shines as far as the west, so will be the coming of the Son of Man...and then all the tribes of the earth will mourn, and they will see the Son of Man coming on the clouds of heaven with power and great glory. (Matthew 24:27)

Christ's second coming is approaching swiftly. The great day of the Lord is near and hastening fast (Zephaniah 1:14). As we pray, God opens the eyes of our faith, and we see his day coming with gathering momentum. Clouds pregnant with justice burst open and cleanse the land. The rains of grace refresh the earth with new life. The storm passes, and a joyous new day dawns as the sun rises to an everlasting day.

Our prayer, indeed the whole Christian life, is filled with this happy expectation. Heartbreaking sorrows, trials, failures, and even sin cannot quench it. The indwelling Spirit of Christ has fixed this hope in the deepest, innermost part of our being. As we pray, we eagerly await the glorious inheritance of the sons of God.

Compare this expectation of Christ's coming kingdom to the constricted and temporary hopes of the world. What a contrast between the believer's expectation and the world's vision of the future! People of this age have fixed their eyes on the here and now. Future visions are filled with apocalyptic anxiety. Strident and desperate voices pound slogans into our collective soul.: "Stop global warming!" "Ban nuclear warfare!" "Win the war against terrorism!"

For the worldly today, joy in creation is supplanted by a fight for survival. Glued to the "news," they watch economic indicators rise and fall, recoil at disasters and tragedies, and are gripped by fear and distress. Men, women, and children are left without hope and without God in the world (Ephesians 2:12).

A day of reckoning precedes the day of renewal.

Jesus' first coming was in weakness and sacrifice; his second coming will be in power and judgment. He came as a lamb to die; he returns as a lion to conquer. In the closing scene of human history, Jesus dominates the horizons of heaven and earth.

> *For as the lightning comes from the east and shines as far as the west, so will be the coming of the Son of Man...and then all the tribes of the earth will mourn, and they will see the Son of Man coming on the clouds of heaven with power and great glory.* (Matthew 24:29-31)

Reckoning precedes renewal. The judgment of all who oppress and enslave the earth must happen for the earth to be set free. The glorious liberty of the sons and daughters of God requires deliverance from their captors. If the slave is to be set free, then the slave owner must first be defeated. This prayer captures God as our liberator:

> *May God defend the cause of the poor of the people, give deliverance to the needy, and crush the oppressor.* (Psalm 72:4)

> *From the heavens, you uttered judgment; the earth feared and was still, when God arose to establish judgment, to save all the humble of the earth.* (Psalm 76:8)

Out of dreadful warnings arises a beautiful invitation. The warning of judgment is simultaneously a call to repentance and faith. God takes no pleasure in the death of the wicked (Ezekiel 33:11). He desires for everyone to be saved. (1 Timothy 2:4) He offers a full and free pardon to all who bow the knee to the coming king. *"The Spirit and the Bride say, 'Come.' And let the one who hears say, 'Come.' And let the one who is thirsty come; let the one who desires take the water of life without price."* (Revelation 22:17) Our job is simple—we get to hand out the wedding invitations (Luke 14:17)!

We pray daily to be prepared for his coming. We pray daily for our neighbor—and the whole world—to come to Jesus in repentance and worship.

We look for signs that his coming is near.

What signs do we look for? How soon will the second coming be? One sign will be a massive turning to Christ. As Jesus foretold, This gospel of the kingdom will be proclaimed throughout the whole world as a testimony to all nations, and then the end will come (Matthew 24:14).

This rapid expansion of the kingdom is happening now! We learn from the book China's Christian Millions that between 1990 and 2010 the number of Chinese Christian believers surged from ten million to seventy million, and the numbers continue to rise. We read in A Wind in the House of Islam how the evangelization of the Muslim world, previously closed for 1,400 years, is now suddenly open. From a mere handful of believers at the turn of the century, there are now more than two million followers of Christ in the Muslim world. It is no coincidence that the international concerted prayer using Thirty Days of Prayer for the Muslim World began in 2000, the turn of the new century. This movement has now swollen to millions of intercessors who pray during Ramadan for the world of Islam. Similar stories of great numbers of conversions to Christ are coming out of India, Southeast Asia, Cuba, South America, and Africa.

Another sign of Jesus' imminent return will be a growing coldness and hatefulness of the world's inhabitants toward one another. Much of this antipathy will be poured out on God's people.

> *Then they will deliver you up to tribulation and put you to death, and you will be hated by all nations for my name's sake. And then many will fall away and betray one another and hate one another. And many false prophets will arise and lead many astray. And because lawlessness will be increased, the love of many will grow cold.* (Matthew 24:9-12)

Today the persecution of believers is a worldwide reality, and the intensity is increasing. In fact, much of the world is arrayed against Christ and his people. There is widespread persecution of Christians in the Islamic world, as well as in China, Cuba, and North Korea. And radical Hindus in India have recently banded against the cause of Christ, exiling foreign missionaries. Moreover, leaders, rulers, and policymakers in the state, judiciary, and public service of the atheistic West institute more and more laws that ignore God's law, forbid the use of his name in public institutions, and otherwise hinder the advance of the gospel.

Psalm 2 is prophetic of our day: *"Why do the nations conspire and the peoples plot in vain? The kings of the earth rise up and the rulers band together against the Lord and against his anointed."* (Psalm 2:1-2) When the nations gather together against Jesus and his people, he tells us to watch, pray, and prepare for his coming.

Another sign that heralds the return of Christ is that the world starts to come apart at the seams.

The earth is utterly broken, the earth is split apart, the earth is violently shaken.... The earth staggers like a drunken man; it sways like a hut; its transgression lies heavy upon it, and it falls, and will not rise again. (Isaiah 24:12-13, 19-20)

Not only fiery street evangelists see the coming of the end; apocalyptic images fill our collective vision of the future. Movies and TV shows forebode a catastrophic and cannibalistic world. Consider Hunger Games, Night of the Living Dead, Planet Z, Legion, Twilight, Mad Max, and The Book of Eli, among countless more examples. We are feeding the coming generations a vision of death and despair. This calls us to pray for our children.

"Come, Lord Jesus!"

In our world today we clearly see the storm clouds gathering on the horizon. The great day of the Lord is near, near and hastening fast (Zephaniah 1:14). A new day is dawning. It demands that God's Word fill our prayers with expectant joy and terrible urgency, that we pray together with all the saints for millions to accept the salvation of the Lord.

An Example from History:
THE FULTON STREET REVIVAL (1857)

Sometimes it is during the days of hopelessness and despair that revival comes. So it was in the middle of the nineteenth century. The United Status during the mid 1800s witnessed a spiritual, political, and economic low point. Agitation over the slavery issue had bred much political unrest, and civil war seemed imminent. To make matters even more tenuous, financial panic hit in 1857. Banks failed, railroads were bankrupt, factories closed, and unemployment increased. Many Christians realized the need for prayer in such dire situations, and prayer meetings began to spread around the country.

A businessman named Jeremiah Lanphier became an outreach pastor in New York City. Lanphier felt led by God to start a weekly prayer meeting in which business people could meet for mid-day prayer. Anyone could attend for a few minutes or for the entire hour. Lanphier rented a hall on Fulton Street in New York City and advertised its availability for prayer meetings.

The first day of prayer on September 23, 1857, Lanphier prayed alone for half an hour. By the end of the hour, six men from at least four denominational backgrounds joined him. Two days later the Bank of Philadelphia failed, and the following week twenty people joined the prayer meeting. On October 7 there were nearly forty in attendance. The meeting was of such blessing to the attendees that they decided to pray together daily. On October 10 the stock market crashed, and the financial panic triggered a religious awakening, in which people flocked to Lanphier's prayer meetings. One week later more than one hundred were in attendance, including many unsaved persons who were convicted by the Holy Spirit of their sin. Within six months, ten thousand people were gathering for daily prayer in New York City!

Within one month pastors who had attended the noon prayer meetings on Fulton Street started morning prayer meetings in their own churches. Soon the meeting places were overcrowded. Men and women, young and old, of all denominations met and prayed together without distinctions. The meetings abounded with love for Christ, hospitality for fellow Christians, passion for prayer, and fervor for witnessing. Those in attendance experienced an awesome sense of God's presence and answers to specific prayers.

Six months later, by March 1858 a theater building opened for prayer, and even before the prayer meeting began, the facility had reached capacity and people were turned away. Hundreds stood outside in the streets because they could not get inside. By the end of March, over six thousand people met daily in prayer gatherings in New York City. Many churches added evening services for prayer, and soon there were nearly two hundred corporate prayer meetings each day across Manhattan and Brooklyn.

Within three months of the start of what became known as the Fulton Street Revival, similar noon-day prayer meetings sprang up all across America—in Boston; Baltimore; Washington, D.C.; Richmond; Charleston; Savannah; Mobile; New Orleans; Vicksburg; Memphis; St. Louis; Pittsburgh; Cincinnati; Chicago; and a multitude of other cities, towns, and rural communities. Often the doors of businesses held signs reading, "Closed, will reopen at the close of the prayer meeting."

News of the prayer meetings and spiritual revival travelled westward by telegraph, such that this was the first revival in which the media played an important role in spreading the revival.

America entered a new period of faith and prayer. Educated and uneducated, rich and poor, business leaders and common workmen—all prayed, believed, and received answers to prayer. Even the President of the United States, Franklin Pierce, attended many of the noon prayer meetings.

Unlike earlier awakenings in history, prayer was the main instrument of this revival. This was not a revival of powerful preaching. This was a movement of earnest, powerful, prevailing prayer.

The prayer meetings were interdenominational in nature and were organized by lay people. The meetings were very informal—any person might pray, exhort, lead a song, or give a testimony, with a five-minute limit placed on each speaker.

Prayers would be requested for unconverted friends and loved ones from all over the country. In a day or two, testimonies would be given of how the prayers had already been answered. In some towns, nearly the entire population repented and turned to Christ for salvation. The Presbyterian Magazine reported that as of May 1858, nearly fifty thousand people converted to Christianity as a result of the revival.

The results of the Fulton Street Revival continued for decades and created long-term fruit in the areas of evangelism, missions, and social action. Many who became Christian leaders during the second half of the nineteenth century were greatly affected by the revival—D.L. Moody, William Booth, C.H. Spurgeon, and A.B. Simpson.

Danielle Severance. *When Revival Ran Epidemic*. (Richmond, VA: Salem Web Network, April 18, 2010). https://www.christianity.com/church/church-history/timeline/1801-1900/when-revival-ran-epidemic-11630508.html

KINGDOM-COME PRAYER TODAY

1. What do your current prayers reveal about your perspective of Jesus? Are they self-involved or God-exalting? How might you "fix your eyes" or alter your vision of Jesus so that your prayers reflect his glorified position as resurrected and exalted King?

2. We are told to be filled with the Spirit. How often do you ask God to immerse you in the reality of Jesus' personal presence and power? How much of your prayers and daily life reflect this reality?

3. What difference would it make to your prayers if you fed your imagination and heart with the grand hope of his imminent coming?

CHAPTER 5

How Holy Spirit Advances Begin in Prayer

The New Testament Sets a Sequence of Mission

When it comes to mission strategy, there is easy agreement that prayer is important. But when it comes to putting our plans into practice, few are willing to make prayer first in priority and first in sequence. A study of the powerful expansion of the early church, however, confirms the primacy of prayer. As we shall see in this chapter, every advance was initiated by prayer.

When prayer is discovered to be central to kingdom advance, we must go back to the drawing board to get in step with the Holy Spirit. For our strategies to be in line with God's Word, we must begin on our knees and immerse all we do in prayer.

Visions that once pulsed with life grow old and wooden unless they are forged, shaped, and reshaped in prayer.

As we pray and plan in prayer, we will be caught in the Spirit's forward momentum and carried into the mission of Christ. When we become tethered to outdated and ineffective mission strategies, only the Holy Spirit can unshackle us.

Some years ago I had a defining moment when I was taught this lesson in a powerful and personal way. Driving to work in Atlanta on the I-85 South, I was heavy with discouragement. I came to Spaghetti Junction, a complex triple-tier intersection, passing underneath several highways overhead. For me, this junction became a metaphor for the many challenges hitting me from all sides over the previous weeks and months.

One of my children was going through some serious growing-up problems, and my heart was wounded for her. Intersecting with this, I was assaulted by doubts regarding the home mission strategy I had been leading for our denomination. We were starting many churches, but some of our finest pastors were failing. Colliding with this was a realization that few of our church starts were effective at reaching and serving those outside the church. We were working hard and praying some, but I couldn't shake the firm conviction that something important was missing. In the center of these troubles, I was seriously considering resigning.

Somewhere between entering the junction and coming out the other side, my conflicting thoughts began to untangle. God was pointing me in a new direction. Over the next weeks it became clear. I knew I needed to change course—I needed to get back to the biblical and Holy Spirit strategy for mission. Above all else, I needed to lead in prayer. I was still sad, but my heavy spirit began to lift.

At the time, I had been studying the book of Acts in my personal reading. I started there and stayed there, which led me to an intensive and in-depth study of this book. The following observations came out of this challenging time.

The Holy Spirit's strategy to reach the world

A survey of the Acts of the Apostles, which is firstly the acts of the Holy Spirit, reveals the central role of prayer in the advance and expansion of the church. The work of the Holy Spirit is always evidenced in a praying people. Leaders and members launch the mission in steadfast prayer (Acts 1:14, 2:1). From united prayer flows bold and sacrificial evangelism (Acts 2:41, 4:3-4). As thousands of people are saved, new believers are enfolded into a praying community (Acts 2:42-47). When the Spirit is in charge, leaders devote themselves to prayer and the Word (Acts 6:4). From prayer-formed fellowship flows everything that is needed to advance the gospel: leaders exercise church discipline (Acts 5:13-14), deploy other leaders (Acts 6:1-7), nurture lay evangelism (Acts 8:4), and champion church planting (Acts 9:31). As leaders and people unite in prayer, the early church enjoys explosive, joyous expansion.

The New Testament sequence

There is a pattern and sequence to the history of kingdom advance. A study of the text reveals an order that is as significant as the events themselves. Luke, the author of Acts, provides the church with a pattern for future mission activity by presenting an intentional chronology. This sequence is not accidental, but normative.

Specifically, the New Testament mission consists of five stages in chronological sequence:

1. The outpouring of Christ's power in the context of waiting prayer (Acts 1:8,14; 2:1-4)
2. Conversion growth through the bold evangelism and the preaching of Christ's resurrection (Acts 2:36-41)
3. Community formation from a harvest of new converts (Acts 2:41-47)
4. Mobilization through leadership selection and lay development (Acts 6:1-8, 8:4)
5. Multiplication through extensive church planting (Acts 9:31)

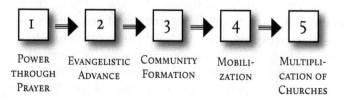

1. Waiting Prayer

The first in both priority and sequence is empowerment through concerted and united prayer. The emphasis is on the disciples waiting: *"Wait for the promise of the Father, which you have heard from me, for John baptized with water, but you shall be baptized with the Holy Spirit not many days from now."* (Acts 1:4) Waiting is obedience translated into prayer.

The disciples have just seen the risen Christ. They are eager and willing to head out, yet they must wait in prayer before proceeding. The coming battle will be hard-pitched and to-the-death, every advance met by counterattack. The disciples are commanded to wait, and so they wait in earnest and united prayer:

> *These all continued with one accord in prayer and supplication, with the women and Mary the mother of Jesus, and with his brothers...Now when the day of Pentecost had fully come, they were all with one accord in one place.* (Acts 1:14, 2:1)

What happens next is proof of the almightiness of the ascended Christ as he answers their prayers with supernatural manifestations:

> *When the day of Pentecost arrived, they were all together in one place. And suddenly there came from heaven a sound like a mighty rushing wind, and it filled the entire house where they were sitting. And divided tongues as of fire appeared to them and rested on each one of them. And they were all filled with the Holy Spirit and began to speak in other tongues as the Spirit gave them utterance.* (Acts 2:1-6)

A time honoured saying is "well begun, half done." This applies to beginning our every endeavor on a foundation of prayer.

2. Bold and Effective Evangelism

Flowing from the headwaters of prayer, the second stage of the Acts model is courageous evangelism that results in a river of conversions. Peter's bold sermon provides an example of the kind of uncompromising preaching that saves souls:

> Let all the house of Israel therefore know for certain that God has made him both Lord and Christ, this Jesus whom you crucified. Now when they heard this they were cut to the heart, and said to Peter and the rest of the apostles, "Brothers, what shall we do?" And Peter said to them, "Repent and be baptized every one of you in the name of Jesus Christ for the forgiveness of your sins, and you will receive the gift of the Holy Spirit...." So those who received his word were baptized, and there were added that day about three thousand souls. (Acts 2:36-41)

Obeying Christ, they wait. As they wait, they receive power. Having received power, they witness—with tremendous results.

Far from being shy about numbers, the early church measured the Spirit's advance in the language of arithmetic: "There were added that day about three thousand souls" (Acts 2:41); "the number of men came to be about five thousand" (4:4); "the number of disciples multiplied and a great many priests became obedient to the faith" (6:7); "more and more the church multiplied" (9:31); "a great many people were added to the Lord" (11:25).

In parallel language, Luke narrates how the gospel message spreads with increasing momentum: "the word of God increased" (Acts 6:7); "the word of God increased and multiplied" (12:24); "the word of the Lord spread throughout the region" (13:49); "so the word of the Lord increased and prevailed mightily" (19:20).

When leaders evangelize, it is contagious. Leaders and people "were all filled with the Holy Spirit and continued to speak the word of God with boldness" (Acts 4:31). After Stephen is martyred, "those who *were scattered went about preaching the word"* (8:4). *"And the hand of the Lord was with them, and a great number who believed turned to the Lord"* (11:21). Like the apostles, God's people become evangelists!

Many Christians today have the will and desire to share their faith. They know the need but are held back by fear. False prophets counsel them to stay put and stay safe: "You might offend someone." A timid flock waits for a few bold leaders to plunge into evangelism; once they dive in, members follow. Yes, some are persecuted for the cause, but this only serves to drive everyone to their knees, pleading for more power. Only the false prophets end up disappointed.

Healings and Deliverance

As well as an abundance of conversions, following the pouring out of the Spirit are a profusion of miracles, mighty acts of deliverance and a torrent of spectacular healings. It would do violence to the Scripture and lessen the comprehensive reality of Christ's saving work if we did not pray eagerly and expectantly for healings, deliverance, special guidance, and other wonderful works of God.

God speaks and acts with power. As long as our prayers are fueled by faith and guided by God's promises, we can be confident that if we ask we will receive.

It is a sad reality that we have often taken our greatest struggles and turned them over to the medical and recovery professions without thought or hope that God can do his great works in answer to prayer, with or without ordinary means. We ask for God to heal someone who is sick or addicted, or pray for deliverance for one who is struggling with mental illness, but all too often our prayers lack faith and expectation. We have given up hope that earnest and united prayer will be followed by the wonders of God through Christ.

Of course, the miraculous and medical are not mutually exclusive. Here is a testimony of how a dear friend experienced deliverance and learned the power and purpose of prayer while in a recovery program.

> From the moment I entered treatment for alcohol and substance abuse and began to practice the Twelve Steps as a program of recovery, I realized that prayer would be a significant aspect of my desire for long-term sobriety. Once sober, I was ashamed to admit that during active addiction, my prayers were mostly selfish and one-sided. I have learned through my renewed desire to delve deeply into the gospel that constant prayer is actually the foundation of my recovery and that I must continue to pray for the salvation of others in order to fulfill God's desire for me and for his kingdom. Kingdom prayer and looking at life through a healthier lens, while actively praying for others, has blessed me with a relationship with my Savior that I had never have dreamed possible. God's authority is at the heart of my resolve to remain sober until I take my last breath.

On the other hand, works of healing and deliverance often bypass ordinary means. In the world of Islam, many thousands are introduced to Christ, Isa, through dreams and visions. God often introduces himself to Hindus in India through healings in answer to the prayers of Christians.

God is pleased to display the splendor of his majesty and the greatness of his might. A First Nations woman from the Maskwacis Reserve in Alberta testified, "I am a Christian for one reason. It is not by going to church. It is because Jesus has far greater power than all the other spirits. Because of his great power, I left those ways behind and became his follower."

3. Community Formation

The third stage in the Spirit's pattern for mission is community formation. All who long for the coming kingdom are awed (and perhaps a little envious) at the description of the first community of believers in Acts 2:42-47 and 4:32-25:

*Those who gladly received the Word were baptized...and they
continued steadfastly in the apostles' doctrine and fellowship, in
the breaking of bread and in prayers...Now all who believed were
together, and had all things in common...breaking bread from
house to house, they ate their food with gladness and simplicity
of heart, praising God and having favor of all the people. And the
Lord added to the church daily those who were being saved.*

The vitality and joy of the New Testament church is directly
proportional to the momentum of prayer and the multiplication
of new converts. A community of love and kindness forms
spontaneously out of the fertile soil of evangelism. The leaders
do not need to organize and promote prayer meetings; they
couldn't keep people from gathering if they wanted to! In
the atmosphere of radical witness we find newly regenerated
believers, amazing deliverance, radiant joy, contagious
selflessness, and sacrificial giving. Nothing can discourage the
fellowship from growing.

4. Leadership Mobilization

Selecting and deploying new leaders is the fourth stage in the
sequence. In the early church, rapid growth opens the door for
new leaders. The twelve disciples are soon overwhelmed by the
legitimate needs of thousands of new believers.

Before long, the opportunity to expand the leadership
presents itself. It comes in the way of a test for the apostles.
Trouble arises from within the fellowship, and the Holy Spirit
provides the solution. The issue is serious; widows are being
neglected in the daily distribution of food. They are Grecian
widows, so there is an implication that Jewish leaders are being
unfair to Gentile converts. Wisely, the apostles make a strategic
decision. They stay on task, expand the leadership base, and
involve the people in the process:

*Now in these days when the disciples were increasing in number,
a complaint by the Hellenists arose against the Hebrews because
their widows were being neglected in the daily distribution. And*

the Twelve summoned the full number of the disciples and said, "It is not right that we should give up preaching the word of God to serve tables. Therefore, brothers, pick out from among you seven men of good repute, full of the Spirit and of wisdom, whom we will appoint to this duty. But we will devote ourselves to prayer and to the ministry of the word." (Acts 6:1-4)

The results are outstanding! To the credit of the Jewish apostles, prayer remains the priority. At the same time the widows receive attention, and the leadership base expands. Seven Greek believers are selected as deacons. These men become outstanding ministers, with Stephen and Philip leading the way. Rather than slowing down, the movement radically expands. As a result, the word of God continued to increase, the number of the disciples multiplied greatly in Jerusalem, and a great many priests became obedient to the faith (Acts 6:7). The church is multiplied and mobilized as never before.

5. Church Multiplication

The final stage of the sequence is church planting. Acts 9:31 reads as a summary and celebration of the first four stages: *"Then the churches throughout all Judea, Galilee, and Samaria had peace and were edified. And walking in the fear of the Lord, and in the comfort of the Holy Spirit, they were multiplied."*

The formation of hundreds of new churches throughout Palestine marks the completion of the first phase of Christ's strategy to reach the world. Prayer precedes empowerment. Bold evangelism births new believers. Converts are united in sacrificial and joyful community. The selection of new leaders mobilizes the church, resulting in the formation of new congregations throughout Judea, Galilee, and Samaria. In every respect, the entire church enters, embraces, and enacts the mission of the Holy Spirit!

Repetition of the sequence in Acts

Each of the five stages in the Spirit's mission plan builds upon the previous one. No stage can be omitted, nor the order altered. For example, without power through prayer, evangelism produces little fruit. Without conversion growth, community formation stalls. This required sequence highlights a weakness in a great many mission endeavors today; an inadequate prayer base results in weak evangelistic efforts and anemic growth. Even if new churches experience numerical growth, too often it can be the result of gathering Christians who leave their previous fellowship to try out something new.

Not only do the five stages build upon each other, but so too must the sequence be continually repeated. This is how the Holy Spirit works. The five stages that initially occur at Pentecost are repeated in striking detail later in Acts (see Acts 4).

After the first wave of advance, the stage is set for a cosmic collision between the church and the very rulers that conspired the death of Christ. The young church has experienced explosive growth. Thousands are coming to Christ, and in so doing are discovering community, healing, and joy. The political and religious powers are alarmed; they realize the movement of Christ is not going to fade away.

> *And as they were speaking to the people, the priests and the captain of the temple and the Sadducees came upon them, greatly annoyed because they were teaching the people and proclaiming in Jesus the resurrection from the dead. And they arrested them and put them in custody until the next day, for it was already evening. But many of those who had heard the Word believed, and the number of the men came to about five thousand.* (Acts 4:1-4)

The enemy hits back, hard. The religious rulers could not accept that the disciples were preaching a crucified and risen Christ and were performing miracles just as he did. They demand of Peter and John, *"By what power or by what name did you do this?"* (Acts 4:7). When they realize that the name and power in question is none other than the same Jesus they crucified, they sharpen their assault: *"But in order that it may spread no further among the people, let us warn them to speak no more to anyone in this name."* So, they called them and charged them not to speak or teach at all in the name of Jesus (4:17).

The response of the church to these threats is telling. Leaders and people go to prayer—but not just any prayer. This is concerted, united, kingdom prayer. They cry out to the King to advance his kingdom:

> *And when they heard it, they lifted their voices together to God and said, "Sovereign Lord, who made the heaven and the earth and the sea and everything in them, who through the mouth of our father David, your servant, said by the Holy Spirit, 'Why did the Gentiles rage, and the peoples plot in vain? The kings of the earth set themselves, and the rulers were gathered together, against the Lord and against his Anointed for truly in this city there were gathered together against your holy servant Jesus, whom you anointed, both Herod and Pontius Pilate, along with the Gentiles and the peoples of Israel, to do whatever your hand and your plan had predestined to take place. And now, Lord, look upon their threats and grant to your servants to continue to speak your word with all boldness, while you stretch out your hand to heal, and signs and wonders are performed through the name of your holy servant Jesus."* (4:24-30)

What follows is, event by event, phrase by phrase, clearly a repetition of the sequence in Chapters 1 and 2:

> *And when they had prayed, the place in which they were gathered together was shaken [Stage 1], and they were all filled with the Holy Spirit and continued to speak the word of God with boldness [Stage 2]. Now the full number of those who believed were of one heart and soul, and no one said that any of the things that belonged to him was his own, but they had everything in common [Stage 3]. And with great power the apostles were giving their testimony to the resurrection of the Lord Jesus, and great grace was upon them all. There was not*

a needy person among them, for as many as were owners of lands or houses sold them and brought the proceeds of what was sold (4:31-34).

Once again, power falls from on high. This time the earth quakes. All the believers are filled (again!), which results in bold evangelism by leaders and people. The community is further strengthened in love, prayer, and good works. Leader mobilization [stage 4] and church planting [stage 5] soon follow.

This repetition of the sequence encourages us to cry out for the Holy Spirit again and again. This earthquake reveals that Pentecost is the epicenter of many empowerments for the church for that day and ours. The pouring out of the Spirit is not a one-time event, nor are the spectacular manifestations of Christ's power only for that day.

Acts 4 is not the only time this pattern is repeated in Acts. In an abbreviated way, this prayer sequence is repeated another six times. We discover that every advance begins with prayer; bold witness follows, and the fellowship grows in numbers and strength.

In Acts 6:1-7, the leaders resolve to devote themselves to prayer and the word. Following this prayer resolve, the leadership base expands, the fellowship is strengthened and conversions multiply.

In Acts 7:60, 8:4 and 11:21 that there is widespread evangelism after the prayer of Stephen. These lay evangelists become the first apostolic witness to the Gentile world! They go to Antioch and lead non-Jews to Christ.

In Acts 9 and 10, Peter's and Cornelius' prayers precede the gospel going to the Gentile world. They are praying about different things at different times and in different situations. Though they are both unaware of it, they are having a prayer meeting which the Holy Spirit uses to break the barrier between Jew and Gentile. Cornelius and his entire household are converted and filled with the Holy Spirit. The leaders of the whole church are mobilized to move ahead with the Spirit's plans to reach the world for Christ.

In Acts 12:5,10, an all-night prayer meeting brings deliverance for Peter, frustrates the enemies of the church, and opens the gates of the city:

> *So Peter was kept in prison, but earnest prayer for him was made to God by the church.... When they had passed the first and the second guard, they came to the iron gate leading into the city. It opened for them of its own accord....*

We can only imagine the joy of this praying community as they discover the power of intercessory prayer.

Acts 13:1-4 highlights how the prophets of Antioch pray their way into the global mission. While they are praying and ministering to God, the Holy Spirit takes charge of the mission. Their little plans meet the great plans of Christ: *"Set apart for me Barnabas and Saul for the work I have called them."* There is an important lesson here. The Holy Spirit reveals his mission strategies as we pray. Apart from prayer, the specific plans of the Holy Spirit remain hidden.

Finally, in Acts 16, Paul and Barnabas are imprisoned in Philippi. As they worship and pray, they experience another mighty earthquake, the prison doors are opened, and the jailer and his household are saved. There will soon be a church family in Philippi. Again, we discover that every advance is initiated by prayer and bold witness—conversions and community formation follow.

A repetitive sequence, but not mechanical

We've outlined the New Testament order, sequence, and repetition of Holy Spirit advances. It should be noted, however, that the work of the Holy Spirit is never mechanical. We witness an interplay of these stages as the Spirit leads the church onward; for example, prayer is part of every stage of the advance, and bold evangelism is continuous and ongoing. Community formation never stops. New leaders emerge and are mobilized at every stage, and churches are planted all along the way.

An enhanced illustration of the five stages of kingdom-advance looks like this:

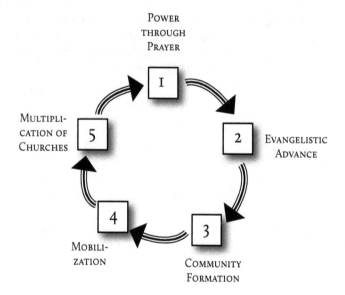

Conclusion

Luke's narration of the repeated sequence is no coincidence. In fact, it is a message from Christ to his church. The sequence of prayer empowerment, bold mission enactment, community formation, leader multiplication, and new church creation will be repeated again and again across the ages. This sequence is a paradigm of the Holy Spirit.

KINGDOM-COME PRAYER TODAY

1. What was new to you about this sequence of Holy Spirit mission? Why is it so important? What is the result of going out of sequence?

2. What does waiting in prayer mean to you? Why do we find it hard to wait in prayer?

3. Considering your particular church or ministry, what is the balance across each of the five stages of Holy Spirit advance?

4. How can we keep prayer a priority in each of the stages?

CHAPTER 6

How Prayer Fuels
a Global Movement

The Prayer Life of the Apostle Paul
Transforms the World

P aul the apostle is no armchair quarterback. He leads his
team from the field of battle. He calls his plays in the
teeth of fierce opposition. He doesn't form his strategies
within the safe, cloistered walls of the study but from the
frontlines of mission.

While journeying from city to city on Roman roads, Paul
writes his letters to those he has brought into the kingdom. He
engages the world head on and builds a team to do the same.
Because he leads from the battlefront, people listen to him. His
teaching is filled with a relevant immediacy. His prayers are filled
with love for the church and burden for the lost world.

How Paul fuels his mission through prayer

Paul tells us the kingdom of God is about power (1 Corinthians 4:20). Prayer empowers gospel ministry. Paul has a ministry of power, because he ministers in prayer. He left no doubt about his mission strategy: from his fourteen epistles, we encounter a staggering number of prayers, prayer requests, and exhortations to pray. Paul prays sixty-five times and refers to prayer another twenty-two times in his letters. This includes forty-five benediction and doxology prayers, along with twenty prayers of blessing. In addition, he writes eleven encouragements to pray, four teachings on how to pray, and seven prayer requests. We tend to think of Paul as a great theologian, but perhaps we ought to think of him instead as a mighty man of prayer.

Paul's specific prayers, infused with gospel theology, permeate his letters. For example, throughout the book of Ephesians we find five prayers of blessing (benedictions), two extensive prayers, two exhortations to pray, and one prayer request.

Paul ministers as much by prayer as by teaching. There is an interplay of prayer and teaching in all of Paul's letters. For example, scattered throughout the brief letters of 1 and 2 Thessalonians are nine prayers of benediction, six intercessory prayers, one exhortation to pray, and two prayer requests.

Benediction and doxology prayers

In the benediction and doxology prayers, Paul both pronounces and invokes God's blessing. Most of these prayers are found at the beginning and end of the letters. However, it is a mistake to skip over these prayers as mere conventions of greeting and salutation. These blessings are rich with the life of the Spirit. Paul is fulfilling the priestly calling of all believers; Aaron was set apart...that he should minister to the Lord and pronounce blessings in his name forever (1 Chronicles 23:13)

Here are some examples of Paul's benediction prayers:

May the God of endurance and encouragement grant you to live in such harmony with one another, in accord with Christ Jesus, that together you may with one voice glorify the God and Father of our Lord Jesus Christ. (Romans 15:5-6)

May the God of hope fill you with all joy and peace in believing, so that by the power of the Holy Spirit you may abound in hope. (Romans 15:13)

The grace of the Lord Jesus Christ and the love of God and the fellowship of the Holy Spirit be with you all. (2 Corinthians 13:14)

May the Lord make you increase and abound in love for one another and for all, as we do for you, so that he may establish your hearts blameless in holiness before our God and Father, at the coming of our Lord Jesus with all his saints. (1 Thessalonians 3:12-13)

Now may the God of peace himself sanctify you completely, and may your whole spirit and soul and body be kept blameless at the coming of our Lord Jesus Christ. He who calls you is faithful; he will surely do it. (1 Thessalonians 5:23-24)

These invocations and benedictions are not mere wishes. The word of prayer has the power to impart the blessing prayed for. As Paul's readers hear and receive these words by faith, they are filled with the Holy Spirit's power and blessing.

Surveying the heft of these prayers, we realize how much richer our prayer life would be, and how much more effective our ministry to others, if we filled our prayers with these priestly pronouncements.

Prayers for the churches

In addition to the benedictions, we find twenty other prayers for the churches in Paul's writings. Consider Ephesians: Prayer is at the heart of this weighty letter. These are not polite one-sentence invocations but instead entire paragraphs devoted to intercession. Two "monster" prayers in Chapters 1 and 3 contain some of the richest doctrine in all of Scripture:

> *I pray...that the God of our Lord Jesus Christ, the Father of glory, may give you the Spirit of wisdom and of revelation in the knowledge of him, having the eyes of your hearts enlightened, that you may know what is the hope to which he has called you, what are the riches of his glorious inheritance in the saints, and what is the immeasurable greatness of his power toward us who believe, according to the working of his great might that he worked in Christ when he raised him from the dead and seated him at his right hand in the heavenly places.* (Ephesians 1:15ff)

Wisdom, revelation, knowledge, and enlightenment—all the words of Greek and Roman philosophy are included in a single prayer—even in a single clause of a larger prayer!

What a treasure is ours through prayer! How great the contrast between Christian spirituality and all others. Surely there is more spiritual substance and heavenly riches in this one verse of prayer than in all the teachings of Deepak Chopra, Dali Lama, and Eckhart Tolle combined! Yet, Paul is not being philosophical. He is being pastoral and intentional, confident that his prayer will impart these supernatural realities to the church.

Today's false prophets offer peace through yogic meditations and mantras. They say, "Your soul's needs will be fulfilled by right breathing, right words, and right postures. The key to happiness is living in the present, the everlasting 'now.'" For them, true happiness depends upon a subjective detachment from the storms of life and the ceaseless cultivation of mindfulness.

By contrast, a Christian is concerned not with "living in the present" but in "living in the Presence." The outcome of this God-orientation is a radical and courageous engagement with the world, not detachment from the storms of life. Through prayer, the peace of God so overwhelms the soul of a believer that he or she is able to rise above the chaos of life and is filled with power to dive into the work of restoring fractured lives in a broken world.

A believer has an entirely different experience of spiritual power and happiness. There is no comparison between the peace that comes from the fortress of God's mighty presence and the peace of inconstant awareness and emotions. Reread the above prayer and you notice the striking difference between Christian and neo-pagan spirituality. A believer's daily security rests on the rock-solid foundation of Christ, not on an inner state. Through simple prayer, Christians experience an objective peace rooted in the power of God and the accomplished reality of Christ's resurrection.

Learning to pray as Paul prayed

Firstly, we are encouraged to pray constantly for believers

> *I have not stopped giving thanks for you, remembering you in my prayer.* (Ephesians 1:16)

> *I thank God, whom I serve, as my forefathers did, with a clear conscience, as night and day I constantly remember you in my prayers.* (2 Timothy 1:3)

Pray to give thanks for other believers

> *We always thank God for all of you, mentioning you in our prayers. We continually remember before our God and Father your work produced by faith, your labor prompted by love and your endurance inspired by hope in our Lord Jesus Christ.* (1 Thessalonians 1:2-3)

> *I thank my God every time I remember you. In all my prayers for all of you, I always pray with joy because of your partnership in the gospel from the first day until now.* (Philippians 1:3-5)

> *First, I thank God through Jesus Christ for all of you, because your faith is being reported all over the world.* (Romans 1:8)

Pray for grace and holiness to abound in each believer and church

May he strengthen your hearts so that you will be blameless and holy in the presence of our God and Father when our Lord Jesus comes with all his holy ones. (1 Thessalonians 3:13)

We pray this in order that you may live a life worthy of the Lord and may please him in every way: bearing fruit in every good work, growing in the knowledge of God. (Colossians 1:10)

Pray for the fellowship, that love may increase

And this is my prayer: that your love may abound more and more in knowledge and depth of insight. (Philippians 1:9)

And I pray that you...know this love that surpasses knowledge, that you may be filled to the measure of all the fullness of God. (Ephesians 3:19)

Pray for believers to grow in spiritual knowledge

I keep asking that the God of our Lord Jesus Christ, the glorious Father, may give you the Spirit of wisdom and revelation. (Ephesians 1:16)

I pray that you may be active in sharing your faith so that you will have a full understanding of every good thing we have in Christ Jesus. (Philemon 6)

Pray that they may be filled with the presence and power of Christ

We pray this in order that you may live a life worthy of the Lord and may please him in every way: bearing fruit in every good work, growing in the knowledge of God, being strengthened with all power according to his glorious might, so that you may have great endurance and patience. (Colossians 1:10-11)

I pray also that the eyes of your heart may be enlightened in order that you may know... his incomparably great power for us who believe. That power is like the working of his mighty strength, which he exerted in Christ when he raised him from the dead and seated him at his right hand in the heavenly realms. (Ephesians 1:18-20)

Imagine if our prayers were filled with blessing like the apostle. We would stop judging each other. It would put an end to advice-giving prayer; instead of fixing others, we would ask God to impart the blessings and Spirit of Christ to one another. We wouldn't close our eyes to the sins and failings of others, but we would pray for fresh convictions flowing from the fullness of Christ's Spirit. Paul was aware of the serious problems and sins in the churches, but that didn't prevent him from pronouncing benedictions upon them. "Blessing prayer" is transformative. As we learn more and more to pray this way, our tendency to be critical will weaken, and our affection and concern for others will expand.

There is great hope here for Christian leadership. Once we begin to follow Paul's example and spend much of our prayer time blessing the church as he did, we will already be fueling a movement. Blessing one another in prayer is contagious and others will stream to join in. Yes, for many, there will need to be a radical realignment of our prayer life. It will be disruptive but the rewards will be infinitely worth it.

Prayer encouragements and instructions

In addition to benedictions and other prayers, Paul adds eleven exhortations and four instructions for Christians to pray. Consider this practical encouragement to the Philippian believers:

> *Rejoice in the Lord always; again I will say, rejoice. Let your reasonableness be known to everyone. The Lord is at hand; do not be anxious about anything, but in everything by prayer and supplication with thanksgiving let your requests be made known to God. And the peace of God, which surpasses all understanding, will guard your hearts and your minds in Christ Jesus.* (Philippians 4:4-7)

Paul pastors the people by encouraging them to bring all their sorrows and trials to God in prayer. Paul takes from his own experiences of answered prayer in difficult, even desperate, times and passes it on.

Good pastors realize that their best pastoring often happens as they pray with others under their care. Hours of advice and counsel are often transcended in a single prayer. God gives wisdom and enlightenment. Prayer brings God into the conversation.

Paul's personal prayer requests

Paul not only prays for the churches, he asks for prayer seven times. Paul fuels his mission to the Gentile world with the prayers of the very churches he helped plant.

In his prayer requests, we notice Paul pray for three things: greater boldness, greater opportunities for evangelism, and spiritual deliverance:

> ...and [pray] for me that words may be given to me that I may open my mouth boldly to make known the mystery of the gospel, for which I am an ambassador in chains: that in it I may speak boldly as I should. (Ephesians 6:19, 20)

> Continue earnestly in prayer...praying also for us, that God would open to us a door for the word...that I may make it manifest as I ought to speak. (Colossians 4:2-4)

> He delivered us from such a deadly peril, and he will deliver us. On him we have set our hope that he will deliver us again. You also must help us by prayer so that many will give thanks on our behalf for the blessings granted... (2 Corinthians 1:10,11)

Notice the object of these requests. Paul asks prayer for himself. Paul asks prayer not so much for the lost he seeks to reach, as for his own effectiveness. This is strategic. Paul has been given the promises. He is the instrument; he knows God can change and empower him. Effective missionary praying begins with praying for the messenger.

It was true then, and it is true today; "If you want to reach a world, ask others to pray for you." We may assume that little lasting fruit happens in us or through us without faithful prayer support.

Mission implications of Paul's prayer requests

First, like Paul, we need always to pray for boldness to share the gospel. God will hear these prayers and give us the courage to lead others to Christ. The implication of Paul's requests is clear. Without prayer, fear rules our hearts. Nothing is more daunting in the Christian life than evangelism. You say you are afraid, and you should be. Paul knew fear too! Yet no one can question his resolve to bring Christ into every conversation. The road from fear to freedom is traversed by prayer, especially as others unite in prayer on our behalf.

> *So when they heard that, they raised their voice to God with one accord and said: "Lord, you are God".... Now Lord, look on their threats and grant to your servants that with all boldness they may speak your word.... And when they had prayed, the place where they were assembled together was shaken; and they were all filled with the Holy Spirit and they spoke the Word of God with boldness. (Acts 4:24ff)*

As someone has noted, "The devil trembles when he sees God's weakest child on his knees."

Second, the doors to a city, town, village, or heart of a friend remain closed until opened by prayer. The gates of the city open "of themselves" after the earnest and united prayer of God's people (Acts 12:5,10).

Like Paul, we can expect great results when we pray with others for open doors.

> *I will tarry in Ephesus...for a great and effective door has opened to me, and there are many adversaries. (1 Corinthians 16:9)*

> *When I came to Troas to preach Christ's gospel, and a door was opened to me by the Lord.... Now thanks be to God who always leads us in triumph in Christ, and through us diffuses the fragrance of his knowledge in every place. (2 Corinthians 2:12-14)*

Third, there will be opposition whenever and wherever we preach the gospel. Like Paul, we will need to pray to be delivered from evil people and evil demons. As we pray, God will deliver us!

*But the Lord stood by me and strengthened me, so that through
me the message might be fully proclaimed and all the Gentiles
might hear it. So I was rescued from the lion's mouth. The Lord
will rescue me from every evil deed and bring me safely into his
heavenly kingdom. To him be the glory forever and ever. Amen.*
(2 Timothy 4:17-18)

At present, there is an increasing urgency to pray for
deliverance from those who oppose the gospel. Around the
world, more and more believers are being imprisoned and
martyred even today. A prayer for deliverance is not a nicety—it
is a necessity. There is a darkly humorous dialogue that has
surfaced from Pakistan. At present, many believers in that
country experience great persecution and many have become
martyrs. Here, one Pakistani Christian encourages another:

*"You say you are being investigated. Be glad you were not
interrogated."*
"You say you were interrogated. Be glad you were not arrested."
"You say you were arrested. Be glad you were not tortured."
"You say you were tortured. Be glad you were not killed."

"You say you were killed. Be glad! You are in heaven!"

Conclusion

In studying the letters of Paul, we see the one overarching
mandate for anyone who desires to be a godly leader or make
a long-term spiritual impact: To be a minister of the Word, we
must minister in prayer. Prayer complements and completes the
teaching. Just as prayer apart from the Word lacks its true aim,
the Word apart from prayer lacks its intended power.

Prayer and Word working together is the key to mission
advance. As an effective leader, Paul ministers as much by prayer
as by teaching. For the apostle, prayer completes the teaching. Paul
turns to prayer again and again to tend the sheep and to advance
the gospel. What teaching cannot accomplish, prayer can.

Most notably, Paul's prayers not only contain the word of
God, these prayers are the Word of God!

KINGDOM-COME PRAYER TODAY

1. Review some of your own prayers. How much of your time and focus is spent praying for God to bless his church?

2. The next time you meet with your group, pray for each other by name for spiritual blessing and growth, for courage in personal spiritual warfare, and for deliverance from evil in the ongoing battle.

3. Pray for leaders in your church—for increasing boldness, for open doors of opportunity, and for spiritual protection and deliverance.

CHAPTER 7

How Prayer Precedes Urban Renewal

The Seeds of the Kingdom Harvest Are Planted by a Praying Church

These men who have turned the whole world upside down.
(Acts 17:6)

T he kingdom of Christ advances in both abrupt and gradual ways. Regardless of the pace, the result is a world turned upside down.

In Old Testament revivals, in the life of Jesus, at Pentecost, throughout the early period of the church, and in all the Pentecost aftershocks reverberating throughout history to awaken spiritual revival, the kingdom comes suddenly, unexpectedly, and in manifest power. Thus, in Acts the kingdom arrives and advances in wind, fire, and earthquake (Acts 2 and 4);

prison doors give way to miraculous release (Acts 12:6, 16:26); and city gates open "by themselves" (Acts 12:10). Behind each tectonic upheaval lies the earnest and united prayers of God's people.

In more normal times between revivals, less visible but equally profound kingdom harvest proceeds wherever Christ is proclaimed and obeyed. The roots of faith's tiny "mustard seed" grow unnoticed until a rich forest of faith sprouts, spreads, and shelters many under its canopy.

Likewise, using another of Jesus' metaphors, after the salt is added, it penetrates the entire offering with preserving and enhancing properties. Still again, once leaven is added, though it starts small, over time the yeast eventually leavens the whole product. Mustard seed, salt, and leaven are metaphors used by Jesus to give illustration to the steady, formidable advance of the kingdom throughout the ages until "the gospel of the kingdom is proclaimed throughout the world" and "until justice is established in all the earth."

From beginnings of spiritual conversions and renewal, societal change is how the leaven and salt of the kingdom work their way into the culture. This is critically important in our day, because if we are honest, the church has little influence on the surrounding culture. We see noble ministries of mercy and faithful churches that have held the fort, but many other Christians and churches have drifted away from lives of prayer and service. At the same time, the city has pushed the church and its saving message to the sidelines. To progress, we must start over.

Hope is not far off. Wherever the good news is sown, the seed begins to grow. When we started Grace Vancouver Church in the heart of the city, our intent was two-fold. First, we would pray and build a praying church. Second, we would ask God to insert us into the heart and artery of the city. As a one visionary colleague put it, "Your church should be so indispensable to the community, that if you were to leave, it would tear the heart out of it."

Over the following years, God answered our prayers and opened doors to the city. An elderly couple fed, gathered, and loved dozens of international students, and others joined in to help. People from all over the world became new believers.

One of our women leaders connected us with a local neighborhood. We partnered with community centre and a Catholic church in the area to start Showers for the Shelterless. A homeless person could park their shopping cart with our "valet service" and receive a hot shower, rich hospitality, a hot breakfast, gallons of coffee, a newspaper, and even some new socks or gloves.

When leaders of a ministry to sexually exploited women started coming to the church, we asked them if they would show us how we could partner with them. When they launched their new ministry in our city called Genesis Vancouver, we worked alongside to renovate space and provide volunteer staff for a day program for women and their children.

A gifted leader in our community gathered the artists and worship team leaders to create a flourishing ministry called Art in the City, Art in the Sanctuary. Twice a year our building was crowded with hundreds who gathered on weekend nights to enjoy the work of Christian and non-Christian artists. Our arts team would choose a theme, and we invited artists to submit paintings, prints, and sculptures that fit the theme. After a rich interplay of city and sanctuary, we invited people to come on Sunday morning to hear a sermon about God, creativity, and the arts. A remarkable multi-nation choir would sing a new song for the city.

From small beginnings, the leaven was working.

Societal changes begin within.

Jesus' use of metaphors highlights the revolutionary new order of the new covenant. Revival in Old Testament kingdom era involved visible changes that filtered down to the entire culture. For example,after public prayers of repentance, kings would remove idols, tear down the places of idol worship, and kill the false prophets. Immediately they would restore legitimate temple service, approved priests, leaders, and liturgy. Righteous and repentant kings would instill judicial and military changes, as well.

In the New Testament, however, we see that spiritual renewal begins in people's hearts. Change begins within—in the inner sanctum of the human heart. The first objective is the renewal of souls, and the means are the sword of the Word and acts of love and kindness:

> *Not by swords loud clashing, not thunder of drums*
> *But with deeds of kindness*
> *The God of mercy comes.*

> *~Lead On O King Eternal, Ernest Sherttleff*

The New Testament community plants the seeds which will reshape the world.

1. The early church is a community of equals.

Following the events of Pentecost, the mustard seed of the gospel proliferates through every branch of society, providing a far-reaching network of branches to sustain social and spiritual renewal for every kind of people. Unlike the existing Jewish socio-religious construct with its centralized government and heredity-based religious class, the newly born church opens its doors to all believers, a remarkable example of a populist movement: *"Here there is not Greek and Jew, circumcised and uncircumcised, barbarian, Scythian, slave, free; but Christ is all, and in all."* (Colossians 3:11)

The powers that be take note: the leaders of this Christ movement are "ordinary men" with no formal training, no pedigree, or education (Acts 4:13), and the community of believers is open to all. Anyone could join the early church, enjoy all its privileges, and even become a prophet or leader. Leaders and people meet together in a common fellowship of prayer, Scripture, and sacrament (Acts 2:42-47). With this kind of open-armed hospitality, is it any wonder that "they found favor with all the people"?

The practice of openness, shared fellowship, and communal helpfulness inspired onlookers to overcome the fear of persecution and join the young church. Despite the fact that joining the early church was a risky proposition, this sharing, loving community proved irresistible:

> *None of the rest dared join them, but the people held them in high esteem. And more than ever believers were added to the Lord, multitudes of both men and women.* (Acts 5:14)

2. The first Christians practice of common property defines generosity for future generations.

While believers had a right to own things, they chose to give much of it away. Although mandated giving was part of the social compact of God's people from their earliest Law-receiving days, this new practice was a departure from the law of tithing. Instead, it was wholly voluntary, representing a new Spirit-led construct of selflessness. It ushered in a social and spiritual revolution of world-changing proportions: *"And all who believed were together and had all things in common. And they were selling their possessions and belongings and distributing the proceeds to all, as any had need."* (Acts 2:42,43)

In Israel and according to God's law, one in every fifty years was called the Year of Jubilee. Throughout the land, all property was to be returned without cost to the original owner.

The best times in any people's history are the periods of human generosity, when the poor are embraced and provided for. In Old Testament times, years of Jubilee ensured rich moments of compassion, restoration, and justice.

In the early church, new believers, set free from their debts to God, act without compulsion and exhibit a new attitude toward their possessions. The principles of Old Testament-mandated Jubilee are spontaneously enacted; property is restored to everyday people—without directive or law (Acts 2:42 and 4:31). This radical practice of extravagant charity begins with the church, but the practice of shared property acts as leaven in every civilization captured by the gospel.

The more Christianity influences a people or society, the greater the generosity and charity. Wherever the gospel of Christ has been preached and received, the result is the establishment of new churches, hospitals, missions, schools, and other ministries of kindness. As a result, institutions for the common good, practices of social justice, and overall societal improvement flourish. One recent example is Serve India: in just eight years, from its beginning in 2009 to 2017, Serve India now works in 23,000 villages throughout India, is training 7,000 church leaders and, at the same time, feeding the hungry and providing education for 12,000 orphans.

3. The early church sets the pattern for representative government.

The early church practices a unique form of representative democracy in which people choose their own leaders. Eventually, centuries later, this seed will grow and reshape statecraft in countries throughout the world.

The episode, found in the sixth chapter of Acts, manifests the enfranchising of common believers, the "liberation of the laity," and the strategic expansion of leadership.

Beyond the twelve apostles, others are elected and appointed by the leaders to provide the care and oversight of the kingdom community.

> *"Brothers and sisters, choose seven men from among you who are known to be full of the Spirit and wisdom. We will turn this responsibility over to them and will give our attention to prayer and the ministry of the word." This proposal pleased the*

whole group. They chose Stephen, a man full of faith and of the Holy Spirit; also Philip, Procorus, Nicanor, Timon, Parmenas, and Nicolas from Antioch, a convert to Judaism. They presented these men to the apostles, who prayed and laid their hands on them. (Acts 6:3-7)

This practice of "choosing from among you" represents a momentous governmental shift from a fixed and hereditary hierarchy to a representative democracy. God's people, for the first time, choose their leaders from their own number, and these new leaders are empowered to act. The unique aspect of Biblical democracy, in contrast with the Athenian "polis," for example, is that church leaders are called not only to act on behalf of the people who vote for them but first of all to represent God before the people.

Following this revolution is the conversion of "a great many priests." (Acts 6:7) Priests were at the heart of that society, so their turning to Christ could not fail to sow the seeds for radical change. Not only so, but it is hardly speculative to imagine that these leaders were deeply affected by this new form of governance. Perhaps these priests had grown fatigued under the religious hierarchy. Regardless, they were hungry for a new order—and found it in the early church.

4. The first Pentecost eliminates racism and tribalism.

The first Pentecost signals a common humanity, as Jews from every nation hear the praises of God in their own language. Another kind of Pentecost happens a few years later in Antioch when this city becomes the epicenter not only of evangelistic advance but also of radical inter-ethnic transformation and community formation. The first "tongues of fire" on the heads of the 120 Jews spread rapidly beyond Palestine. Burning away the old barriers of tribe and tongue and making way for a new multiethnic expression of the people of God, the flames of revival sweep ever outward into the Gentile world.

As things ignite in Antioch of Syria, we notice the typical effect of gospel advance—*"a great many turn to the Lord."*

However, another brief but world-changing phrase is added this time, and in Antioch, *"the disciples were first called Christians."* (Acts 11:26)

This new word for disciples of Jesus heralds the beginning of a global revolution! Antioch was a walled city—not only on the perimeter but also within its outer walls—populated by a multiethnic mix of Syrians, Greeks, Romans, and Jews, with each tribe occupying its own walled quarter.

As the disciples multiply greatly in Antioch, they begin to meet frequently. The result is the formation of a multiethnic Christian community of Syrians, Greeks, Romans, and Jews. Up to now, primary loyalty and identity has been connected with individual tribe ("Paul, a Jew from Tarsus," for example). But these disciples have been given a new identity by a new King, and the result is a new kind of deep and permanent communion with one another that transcends their tribe. The only way for the rest of the city to identify this new, multiethnic, radically-bonded community is to give them a new name—"Christians."

Jesus said that his church would become a city set on a hill. In Antioch, this promise is fulfilled. The Christians in Antioch were fulfilling this word of Christ—in effect, Christians became a city within the city, and the world would never be the same.

5. Gospel encounters lay depth charges to the existing religious and social order.

When Philip preaches the gospel in Samaria, God grants a dramatic display of Holy Spirit power: *"Unclean spirits, crying out with a loud voice, came out of many who had them, and many who were paralyzed or lame were healed."* (Acts 8:7)

Far from these conversions being a private religious experience, the breaking in of the kingdom in Samaria was manifest and widespread. We read the postscript: *"So there was much joy in that city."* (Acts 8:8)

The apostle Paul had an urban strategy for mission. He went to the leading cities of a region, boldly announcing the gospel. This included Antioch, Corinth, Ephesus, Philippi, Athens, and Rome.

Consider Paul's mission to the city of Philippi. When Paul casts out the "spirit of a python" indwelling a slave girl, it brings religious and civil unrest to the entire city. This slave girl was a fortune-teller who brought a great deal of profit to her captors, and the exorcism provokes a violent civic reaction: "These men are Jews, and they are disturbing our city." Paul and Barnabas have intruded the faith into the marketplace and are attacked by the merchant class, and, for this, they are beaten and imprisoned by the governing authorities.

Upon release from prison, the apostles move on to Thessalonica. Once again, their preaching causes social, religious, and political uproar: *"These men who have turned the world upside down have come here also..."* (Acts 17:6) They formed a mob, set the city in an uproar.

After Thessalonica, Paul and Barnabas move onward to Athens. Here Paul gets an audience at the supreme place of public debate and discourse, the Areopagus. Paul preaches to the philosophers of the time. He understands that this place and these thinkers are at the heart of Greek culture, yet he does not use a philosophical argument—he takes on the idols of the land. The invariable aim of kingdom advance is the exposure and overthrowing of the idols of the city. Being then God's offspring, we ought not to imagine that the divine being is like gold or silver or stone, an image formed by the art and imagination of man. The times of ignorance God has overlooked.... (Acts 17:29 ff) Leave idols in place, and nothing changes. Overthrow the idols, and you transform the culture.

Next, we find Paul in Ephesus. With Old Testament force and rapidity, the city is shaken to its foundations. Paul heals and preaches, and God acts in might and miracle. This precipitates a massive reaction of public repentance:

*And God was doing extraordinary miracles by the hands of
Paul.... And fear fell upon them all, and the name of the Lord
Jesus was extolled. Also, many of those who were now believers
came, confessing and divulging their practices. And a number of
those who had practiced magic arts brought their books together
and burned them in the sight of all. And they counted the value
of them and found it came to fifty thousand pieces of silver. So
the word of the Lord continued to increase and prevail mightily.*
(Acts 19:11 ff)

If someone chooses to renounce their religious practices
today, it can go almost unnoticed. A secular life waits in the
wings. In the fused socio-political, religious, and economic world
of that day, however, nearly all people—merchants, government
officials, and religious rulers—are incensed by this public
book burning. Religious, political, and economic forces unite,
infuriated by the intrusion of the message of Christ as Lord:

*About that time there arose no little disturbance concerning
the Way. For a man named Demetrius, a silversmith, who
made silver shrines of Artemis, brought no little business to the
craftsmen. These he gathered together, with the workmen in
similar trades, and said, "Men, you know that from this business
we have our wealth. And you see and hear that not only in
Ephesus but in almost all of Asia this Paul has persuaded and
turned away a great many people, saying that gods made with
hands are not gods...."*

*When they heard this they were enraged and were crying out,
"Great is Artemis of the Ephesians!" So the city was filled with
the confusion.... Now some cried out one thing, some another,
for the assembly was in confusion, and most of them did not
know why they had come together....* (Acts 19:21 ff.)

Here we have powerful proof that earnest prayer and public
preaching of the gospel is never simply a "spiritual event."
Kingdom prayer and bold preaching always penetrate the
foundations undergirding any city or society.

Historians have recorded the inexorable advance of Christ's
kingdom in the decades and centuries following the early church

era. Prayer and evangelism sow the seeds of change. Deepening roots are revealed by bold witness, courageous martyrdoms, and noteworthy exploits of self-giving Christian believers (such as nursing victims of plague and reclaiming unwanted infants from the garbage heaps). As pastors educate the illiterate poor to teach them the doctrines of the faith, the tree sprouts, grows, and bears lasting fruit. Eventually, as barbarian hordes multiply, the church sends missionaries to establish mission outposts throughout the world. Pagan leaders send their children to be educated by the missionary monks, and thousands are converted. The truth marches on.

Contrary to popular thinking, it would take more than the barbarian hordes to overthrow Rome. It would be that little stone, cut from a mountain, that would shatter the giant statue of bronze, with its iron and clay feet.

And in the days of those kings the God of heaven will set up a kingdom that shall never be destroyed, nor shall the kingdom be left to another people. It shall break in pieces all these kingdoms and bring them to an end, and it shall stand forever, just as you saw that a stone was cut from a mountain by no human hand, and that it broke in pieces the iron, the bronze, the clay, the silver, and the gold. (Daniel 2:44,45)

The beast that shreds and tears would lose its teeth in the wake of the terror and splendor of the advancing kingdom of Christ.

An Example from History: JOHN WESLEY AND GEORGE WHITEFIELD (1739)

Consider just one revival in the ongoing history of the church that proved to be light, salt, and leaven for an entire nation. It was the New Year 1739, and the despised Methodists, some 60 or 70 in number, met for a "love feast" of Holy Communion and prayer. Here is John Wesley's account of what happened:

About three in the morning, as we were continuing in prayer, the power of God came mightily upon us, insomuch that many cried out for exceeding joy, and many fell to the ground (overcome by the power of God). As soon as we recovered a little from the awe and amazement at the presence of his majesty, we broke out with one voice, "We praise Thee, O God; we acknowledge thee to be Lord."

God gave these men the assurance that he was going to do something beyond all expectation. A week later, at the age of twenty-two, George Whitefield was ordained, and shortly thereafter he gave his first public sermon in Kingwood, England (a rather barbaric mining town). He preached his first message to 200 people; the next day, 5,000 turned out. A day later, 20,000 came to hear him. At times the entire mass wept with conviction. As Wesley recalled, "White gutters made by tears plentifully fell down their black cheeks as they came from the coal pits."

The early ignition following the Wesley-Whitefield alliance in 1739 takes time to gain force and change the surrounding world. Societal reform following awakenings is gradual. Like leaven, it starts small and takes time, but before long penetrates the whole. William Wilberforce's emancipation directive occurred nearly a century after that first outpouring (from 1739 to 1833).

Yet, the seeds of social renewal were evident from the very beginning.[1] Wesley said, "There is no Christianity that is not a social Christianity." Expelled from the church, the despised Methodists went to the neglected and destitute places of the realm. They preached in the gin alleys, prisons, and madhouses. Where they preached, they sowed seeds of mercy, justice, and good works. Wesley took a humorous view of things. He wrote, "We are forbidden to go to

Newgate [a prison] for fear of making them wicked, and to Bedlam [an insane asylum] for fear of making them mad."[1]

Wherever they preached, the Methodists left blankets as well as Bibles. When a jailer was converted, desperate conditions were immediately addressed. Christian captors began to show kindness to the captives. Social and political changes of all kinds began to take shape.[2]

These seeds of renewal reap a harvest years later in a prison at Bristol. Many of the inmates were French prisoners of the Seven Years' War. Here is Wesley's account:

> About eleven hundred of them were confined in that little place, without anything to lie on but a little dirty straw, or anything to cover them but a few foul thin rags, either by day or by night they died like rotten sheep. I was much affected, and preached that evening on [Exodus 23:9] "Thou shalt not oppress a stranger; for ye know the heart of a stranger, seeing ye were strangers in the land of Egypt" 24 pounds were contributed the next day. With this we bought linen and woolen cloth, which were made into shirts, waistcoats and breeches...all of which were carefully distributed where there was greatest want. Presently after, the Corporation of Bristol sent a large quantity of mattresses and blankets. And it was not long before contributions were set on foot at London and in various parts of the kingdom.

In the London Chronicle, Wesley wrote of the remarkable transformation at Bristol's prison. It was now clean and

---

1   For example, George Whitefield was tireless in raising support for an orphanage in Savannah Georgia. However, this good work was tarnished by Whitefield's endorsement of the slavery that he saw as necessary to support the Bethesda orphans. Ryan Reeves. "George Whitefield Founds an Orphanage." (Austin, TX: The Gospel Coalition, March 25, 2016) https://www.thegospelcoalition.org/blogs/ryan-reeves/history-today-george-whitefield-founds-an-orphanage/

2   Jeffrey, Ibid.

neat, with "no fighting or brawling," there was an unprecedented system of equitable arbitration for prisoners; drunkenness, prostitution, and abuse had been eliminated. Women prisoners were separated from the men. Tools and materials were provided to allow for productive employment, and payment made to prisoners from profits on goods sold. There were regular church services, Bibles had been distributed, and free medical services were available. The keeper who brought all these reforms into effect was a Mr. Dagge, an early convert of the Methodists preaching in his own prison.[3]

The seed was sown, the leaven mixed. The movement of God's Spirit had begun, and the world would never be as it was before. J. R. Green, in his Short History of the English People, wrote that over the ensuing decades:

> "[the revival] changed the whole tone of English society…. The Anglican church was restored to new life and activity. Religion carried to the hearts of the people a fresh spirit of moral zeal, while it purified our literature and manners. A new philanthropy reformed our prisons, infused clemency and wisdom into our penal laws, abolished the slave trade, and gave the first impulse to popular education."[4]

---

3 Jeffrey, Ibid.
4 John Richard Green. *A Short History of the English People.* (Palala Press, 2016).

Kingdom come prayer today

1. First of all, ask God to pour out a spirit of prayer on your church and the churches of your city.

2. Second, pray for "a great number" to turn to the Lord. Out of swelling rivers of new converts, a tide will build to overturn the existing order.

3. Third, ask God how you can sow kingdom seed by marrying acts of justice and kindness with bold and faithful evangelism.

Kingdom Prayer
Breaks Through

CHAPTER 8

How a Nation is Renewed Through Repentance

The Movement Starts Here

Hope for national revival rarely emerges as a discussion point among Christians today. Perhaps our dim view of the future explains it, or perhaps we are reading the Bible more like a history book than a living Word that speaks truth and sparks revival. Many forecast a gloomy tomorrow, but when we turn the pages of the Bible we find that revival is often only a prayer away.

This chapter will uncover five national revivals in the Old Testament kingdom era, in which we will see that each awakening is initiated with repentant prayer. As leaders and people acknowledge and turn from their sins, God answers these prayers; the result is a swelling tide of joy and righteousness filling the land.

In each revival, repentance precedes renewal, just as emptying precedes filling. Those who long for national revival gather together and pray. No detours or shortcuts exist for the healing of our nations; national healing begins with united, humble prayer.

National awakenings always begin with heart-rending repentance of God's people, the church. God calls his people to confess their own sins, even before they pray on behalf of the nation. *"If my people who are called by my name humble themselves, and pray and seek my face and turn from their wicked ways, then I will hear from heaven and will forgive their sin and heal their land."* (2 Chronicles 7:14)

After beginning with deep repentance and confession, we move forward in intercession for our nation. To intercede means to pray on behalf of. We cannot expect a lost world to pray for itself; God's people must take the initiative. We must be the "chief repenters" for the nation. It is not enough to point out and decry the evils of the day; we need to intercede—to repent on behalf of our fellow citizens and to recognize our own complicity in the national sin. When we pray for our nation and its cities, we identify with our fellow citizens and confess "our wicked ways." Judgment begins with the people of God—so does revival.

Intercession for our nation today

How do we pray 2 Chronicles 7:14 today? Often national prayer today starts and finishes by thanking God that we are in a free country as we ask him to bless us with continued prosperity. In other words, we ask God not to disrupt the existing order, but to bless and prosper the status quo. There is little awe of God and a distinct absence of repentance. We seldom intercede for those who feel the sting of poverty, the lash of injustice, or the pain of oppression. This is not kingdom prayer.

In fact the Scriptures have a great deal to say about how we should pray for our land and repent of its sins.

We pray for God to bless those who rule and govern in church, state, courts, and centers of education, that they might establish and enforce just laws, that they might labor for peace, in order that we might live godly lives and that the gospel might advance and prosper in our land. (1 Timothy 2:1-4).

Yet, Christians do not pray for a mere continuance of the current secular state of our nation. Prayer to live a godly life, crying out for the advance of the gospel and the free proclamation of the truth are embedded within the scope of kingdom prayer for our land. As we shall see in the following Biblical examples, heartfelt repentance by the people of God marks the headwaters of rivers of national revival.

If we follow the guideline of 2 Chronicles 7:14, there is no danger of finger pointing and self-righteous accusation when we pray for leaders and against evil in our land. God's Word to Solomon provides the perfect solution. As we intercede for our nation, we confess "our" sins and wickedness and identify with those we pray for. (See Ezra 9, Nehemiah 9, and Daniel 9 as models for how these righteous leaders prayed corporately for their nation).

How lasting hope and deep joy begins with prayer

The time from King Saul to the Babylonian captivity is considered the era of Kings. Second Chronicles starts at the beginning of King Solomon's reign and narrates centuries of national revival. Revival history begins with Solomon's majestic prayer for the nation at the temple dedication.

After King Solomon is established in royal splendor, having inherited a period of peace from his warrior-father, King David, he designs, erects, decorates, and dedicates a stunning temple as the first permanent worship center to Jehovah God. The prayer of dedication offered at its grand opening becomes a prayer for the ages. King Solomon prays not only for the people of his day but also for Israel throughout its history.

In his prayer, Solomon prophesies the inevitable judgments resulting from the neglect of God and his law—drought, famine, plague, defeat in battle, exile into captivity. Solomon pleads with God, asking that, no matter how far his people have strayed, God will hear their humble and repentant prayer and restore them to life and joy.

Here is a summary of Solomon's prayer for the nation:

If there is famine in the land, if there is pestilence or blight or mildew or locust or caterpillar, if their enemies besiege them in the land at their gates, whatever plague, whatever sickness there is, whatever prayer, whatever plea is made by any man or by all your people Israel, each knowing his own affliction and his own sorrow and stretching out his hands toward this house, then hear from heaven your dwelling place and forgive ...

when a foreigner...comes and prays toward this house, hear from heaven your dwelling place...in order that all the peoples of the earth may know your name and fear you....

If they sin against you— for there is no one who does not sin... so that they are carried away captive to a land far or near...if they repent with all their mind and all their heart....and pray toward the city that you have chosen and the house I have built for your name, then hear from heaven your dwelling place their prayer and their pleas, and maintain their cause and forgive your people who have sinned against you. (2 Chronicles 6)

God's answer to Solomon's prayer

As soon as Solomon finishes his prayer—and amid a chorus of trumpet-heralding priests and jubilant singers—God answers Solomon's prayer with the burning glory of his presence. Fire comes down from heaven and consumes the burnt offering and the sacrifices. Then God's splendor and presence fills the temple to overflowing: "*And the priests could not enter the house of the Lord, because the glory of the Lord filled the Lord's house..."* (2 Chronicles 7:1-3) What a remarkable scene of God's pleasure and presence, a foreshadowing of the future great day when the temple will be shaken again, once and for all, when the final sacrifice is offered at nearby Calvary!

Pleased with Solomon's prayer of dedication and intercession, God speaks a promise for the ages, guaranteeing national revival from the very day that his people turn from their sin in repentant prayer: *"If my people who are called by my name humble themselves, and pray and seek my face and turn from their wicked ways, then I will hear from heaven and will forgive their sin and heal their land."* (2 Chronicles 7:14)

God promises forgiveness and healing; for these things to occur, however, there must first be repentance. Repentance is a matter of the heart. In biological terms, the arteries of the human heart become clogged with foreign and pathological elements. At some point life-giving blood can no longer flow through, and radical, open-heart surgery remains the final option and only hope. In the same way, the arteries of a nation become blocked by unrepentant sin. Idolatry in its various forms—sexual immorality of all kinds, neglect of the poor, corruption, bribery, murder, greed, and envy—clog the arteries of national health and strangle life of its joy and meaning. Eventually,

EVALUATING KINGS OF JUDAH
☐ GOOD ☐ BAD ☐ MIX OF GOOD & BAD
Solomon
Rehoboam
Abijam
Asa
Jehoshaphat
Jehoram
Ahaziah
Athaliah queen
Joash
Amaziah
Azariah (uzziah)
Jotham
Ahaz
Hezekiah
Manasseh
Amon
Josiah
Johoahaz (Shallum)
Jehoiakim
Jehoiachin
Zedekiah

death is imminent. The only hope is radical, open-heart surgery: *"I will give you a new heart, and a new spirit I will put within you."* (Ezekiel 36:26)

This pattern of intercessory prayer and God's gracious response repeat throughout Israel's history. King after king and prayer after prayer echoes the spirit of Solomon's petition. When righteous kings "call upon the Lord," and the people "cry out to God" in repentance, God answers their prayers and sends the promised healing. Idols are dismantled, fear of the Lord reinstated, and joy of God's people fill the land.

Prayer revivals in the kingdom era

Sadly, Solomon's revival is brief and followed by a steep decline. In his old age, Solomon leads the nation into worshiping other gods. His son Rehoboam hastens the fall: *"When Rehoboam established his reign, he abandoned the law of the Lord, and all Israel with him."* (2 Chronicles 12:1) Rehoboam's arrogance precipitates the divided kingdom, and his rule is one of pure rebellion, as he casts off all God's commands, *"more than all their fathers had done."* (1 Kings 14:22) He leaves a legacy of idolatry, oppression, and cult prostitution. His son Abijam continues in his father's footsteps.

Revival under King Asa

After twenty years of decline under Rehoboam and Abijah, a prayer revival arises again, this time from King Asa. A crisis precipitates the awakening. Confronted by an innumerable army, King Asa calls upon the Lord, as the odds appear hopeless:

> Asa cries to the Lord his God, *"O Lord, there is none like you to help, between the mighty and the weak. Help us, O Lord our God, for we rely on you, and in your name we have come against this multitude. O Lord, you are our God; let not man prevail against you."* (2 Chronicles 14:11)

God answers Asa's prayer, and the enemy is routed without drawing a sword or throwing a spear. The only work left for the army is to gather the spoils. Strengthened by the words of a prophet, Asa helps the nation bear the fruit of repentance. He proceeds to rebuild what Rehoboam and Abijam destroyed—removing the idols, restoring temple worship, and renewing the covenant. Justice and mercy meet, and joy is restored:

> *They swore an oath to the Lord with a loud voice and with shouting and with trumpets and with horns. All Judah rejoiced over the oath, for they had sworn with all their heart and had sought him with their whole desire, and he was found by them.*
> (2 Chronicles 15:14)

The Jewish people enjoy rest from their enemies as the fires of grace warm the land for the next thirty-five years.

Today revival looks similar, but the path is different. The church is not called to wipe out an earthly army. Our warfare is not with gunfire or horsepower, yet it is still military in nature. The enemies we face each day are the opponents of the gospel and the unseen forces that lead people away from hope and God. Our weapons are power-filled words of witness and Spirit-forged works of kindness and mercy. Chief in a believer's arsenal is prayer.

Lead on, O King eternal,
till sin's fierce war shall cease,
and holiness shall whisper
the sweet amen of peace.
For not with swords' loud clashing
or roll of stirring drums
with deeds of love and mercy
the heavenly kingdom comes.[1]

For not with swords' loud clashing
or roll of stirring drums
with deeds of love and mercy
the heavenly kingdom comes.[1]

---

[1]   Ernest W. Shurtleff (1887), "Lead On, O King Eternal"

Revival under King Jehosophat

This spiritual revival continues, as Asa's son Jehosophat improves upon his father's prayer and resolve: *"He sought the God of his Father and walked in his commandments.... His heart was courageous in the ways of the Lord. And furthermore, he took the high places and Asherim out of Judah."* (2 Chronicles 17:1-6)

When "a great multitude" wages war against the nation, like his father, Jehosophat turns to God in prayer. His words recall Solomon's prayer and God's promise. On this day, not only the king, but everyone in the land, including the priests, temple servants, and singers, along with all the people of Judah, call out to God in mighty prayer and praise:

> *We built for you a sanctuary for your name, saying, "If disaster comes upon us, the sword, judgment, or pestilence, or famine, we will stand before this house and before you—for your name is in this house—and cry out to you in our affliction, and you will hear and save." ...Meanwhile all Judah stood before the Lord, with their little ones, their wives, and their children... Then Jehoshaphat bowed his head with his face to the ground, and all Judah and the inhabitants of Jerusalem fell down before the Lord, worshiping the Lord. ... and the Levites...stood up to praise the Lord, the God of Israel, with a very loud voice... And when they began to sing and praise, the Lord set an ambush...*

The enemy is defeated without a casualty. A lasting peace sets in. Once again the city knows peace and the temple experiences revival: *"...returning to Jerusalem with joy, for the Lord had made them rejoice over their enemies. They came to Jerusalem with hearts lyres and trumpets, to the house of the Lord... So the realm of Jehoshaphat was quiet, for God gave him rest all about."* (2 Chronicles 20:27-30)

More than a century of decline

Following Jehoshaphat's reign, an extended period of spiritual decline ensues. During the next fifteen years, under Kings

Jehoram, Ahaziah, and Queen Athaliah, a spiritual winter sets in. These royals halt the revival and plummet Judah to new depths of idolatry and degradation, such that for the next 130 years only a few brief periods of renewal occur.

This era of death comes to its terminus with King Ahaz, who famously casts off all restraint. In an all-out show of contempt for the Holy one of Israel, he outdoes even the original nations of Canaan in immoral acts and social evil. Ahaz worships Baal, practices child sacrifice, and even sacrifices his own sons *"...according to the abominations of the nations whom the Lord drove out before the people of Israel."* (2 Chronicles 28:3) God gives up Ahaz and Judah to their enemies; tens of thousands are slaughtered in battles with Syria and Samaria, and even more are taken captive.

Still, there is a beautiful redemptive story within this depressing account of national and spiritual mayhem. After winning a battle, the soldiers of the northern kingdom of Israel capture a great crowd of the people of Judah. They lead their fellow Jews chained and naked into captivity. They intend to make slaves of them, but God intervenes and sends a prophet who warns them against their intent to imprison their fellow citizens. Israel heeds God and repents; instead of imprisonment, they provide their brothers and sisters with food and clothing, anoint them with healing oil, and send them home with gifts and provisions (2 Chronicles 28:4ff).

The stage is now set for the greatest king and the greatest awakening since Solomon. Hezekiah, son of Ahaz, will offer a prayer that leads the nation into a great revival.

Awakening under King Hezekiah

From the day he becomes king, Hezekiah sets his heart to follow God. He cleanses the temple of its idols, restores temple worship, and renews the covenant by celebrating the Passover. Joy springs up from the city streets and prayers ascend to heaven: *"So there was great joy in Jerusalem, for since the time of Solomon, the son of David king of Israel there had been nothing like this in Jerusalem... and their voice was heard and their prayer came to his holy habitation in heaven."* (2 Chronicles 30:26-27)

Then one day, some years later, there is a watershed event that precipitates a mighty renewal. Hezekiah and the city of Jerusalem are surrounded by the greatest army in the world. Assyria has set its sights on Jerusalem (see Isaiah 36-39). King Sennacherib of Assyria besieges Jerusalem and mocks God: *"He wrote letters to cast contempt on the Lord, saying, 'Like the gods of the nations who have not delivered their people from my hands, so the God of Hezekiah will not deliver his people from my hand."* (2 Chronicles 32:16,17)

Hezekiah does not respond to Sennacherib; rather, he responds to God: *"Then Hezekiah the king and Isaiah the prophet, the son of Amoz, prayed because of this and cried to heaven...."* (2 Chronicles 32:20-23) God answers in majesty and power. As with previous revivals, the battle is won without a single weapon! The Assyrians are scattered, and Sennacherib killed by his own sons. The land receives peace, and for the next thirty years justice and righteousness flow like a river.

A sixty-year decline

Following Hezekiah, Mannasah and King Amon lead the nation into a six-decade night of sin and shame. During this dark age the nation returns to its godless and lawless ways. Only a few dutiful priests remain. The temple lies neglected. The book of God's law gathers dust. The nation falls back into idolatry, child sacrifice, temple prostitution, occult practices, neglect of the needy, and oppression of the poor (2 Chronicles 33:1-6). Repentance is missing, and every form of sin clogs the nation's heart until the land dies.

Revival under king Josiah

Yet, God is not through with his people—his loving kindness endures forever. God raises up a young man to intercede on behalf of the nation: *"At age 16, while yet a boy, Josiah began to seek the Lord."* (2 Chronicles 34:3) God is pleased with Josiah's prayer, and his answer is immediate. A message of hope comes through Huldah, the prophetess:

> *Because your heart was tender and you humbled yourself before God when you heard his words against this place and its inhabitants, and you have humbled yourself before me and have torn your clothes and wept before me, I also have heard you.... (2 Chronicles 34:23-28)*

Cheered by this word, Josiah brings the nation into a covenant renewal ceremony. The people gladly join the revival. A joyous Passover reflects the national heart of repentance: *"No Passover like it had been kept in Israel since the days of Samuel the prophet."* (2 Chronicles 35:18,19) As with every previous revival, God's challenge and promise in 2 Chronicles 7:14 again come to pass. Josiah and the people confess their wickedness and turn from their sin, and God heals the land. Praise fills the temple and the city. God is worshipped, and justice is restored. The nation resounds with rejoicing.

Applying 2 Chronicles 7:14 to today

One prominent application for us today arises from the preceding history: That deep and tearful repentance signals the beginning of great awakenings. There will be no national revival in our day until God's people unite in humble, repentant prayer. Wherever and whenever the people heed God's call to repentance, the promise of national revival has already begun.

What about the state of Christianity in our nations today? Do we acknowledge the need for widespread repentance in our day? Are things that bad? We might look back at the godless, lawless people of Kings and Chronicles and be rightfully horrified, yet a closer examination reveals parallels that are impossible to ignore. For example, not unlike the six-decade decline before Josiah, we can look back at the church in Canada over the past sixty years and see a steady decline into darkness. If we have the honesty and courage to face it, it is a bleak picture.

In our day, no less than in Josiah's day, the knowledge of God and his Word have been gathering dust. More than half of Canadians attended church in 1960; that number is less than fifteen percent today. Many church attendees goers are believers in name only, attending church less than twice a month. Prayer meetings are empty. In the home Scripture reading and prayer are mere relics of a once robust Christian faith. When we do pray, our prayers are weak in worship and often turned in on ourselves. They exhibit little intercession and no repentance for our sins and our nation. We pray to God as if it is his responsibility to serve us rather than us serve him. It is rare to find prayer for world mission and for the persecuted church. Sunday morning churchgoing has replaced a vital Christianity. We look a lot like Israel in decline.

If the church is in trouble, so is the nation

If we overlay the world of Judah's decline over our world today, we find many parallels. In that day, they worshiped idols. While we do not have statues to misrepresent God, we passionately worship our own inventions. Our idols and attachments are not overtly religious in nature, but they are religious in observance. Our devotion to entertainment and our reverence for technology could well be called the new idolatry. We create an infinite variety of ways to devote our every spare moment to *"the lust of the flesh, lust of the eyes and pride of life."* (1 John 2:16)

Although we may not overtly worship false gods, we ignore God altogether. Step by step, decree by decree, the knowledge of God is being edited from our collective mind. Portrayed as neutral, our secular practices have become a cover-up for mere atheism. To be an atheist, by definition, is to be godless. Atheism in our day often expresses itself as contempt for anyone foolish enough to believe in God or affirm his righteous laws.

The wicked kings of Judah practiced child sacrifice, killing their own children to satisfy the devouring gods they worshiped. For decades, we have allowed unrestricted abortion of unborn children. In Canada, at present, applicants for certain government grants have to sign a document supporting abortion or be denied funding. Beginning in June 2017, Canada now permits the killing of the aged and infirm. In the province of British Columbia, hospital policies prohibit their employees from advising assisted suicide applicants against taking their own life. Within the first seventeen months of legalizing physician-assisted suicide, more than two thousand Canadians were killed by medical procedure!

The Israelites were guilty of sexual sin. They implemented temple prostitution, practiced religious orgies, and committed adultery on a massive scale. In Canada we say sexual practices are a "private matter" and seek to keep the government out of the bedroom. In the process, we close our eyes to adultery and promiscuity. Women, girls, men, and boys are exploited and trafficked into pornography and prostitution. Countless numbers, from the youngest age, are addicted to pornography. We dismiss God's created order for gender distinction as we embrace, promote, and legislate personal gender selection.

When evil kings took over Judah, false prophets praised the existing order and maintained the corrupt system. Today, news media in its various forms provides the propaganda which flatters our way of life and serves the status quo of commerce and politics.

The root nature of our wickedness

One way to describe sin is to say that *each one has gone his own way.* Freedom in our time and place merely means self-determination. We despise any infringement on our autonomy.

In consequence, we become godless and lawless: this is the root "wickedness" referred to in 2 Chronicles 7:14. This is our legacy of sin and justification for God's wrath. And this is why we need national repentance.

We have rebelled against God's law. We live in a glass house and have no right to throw stones at anyone. God's call to repentance and the promise of healing speaks as loudly today as it did in Old Testament times: *"If my people who are called by my name humble themselves, and pray and seek my face and turn from their wicked ways, then I will hear from heaven and will forgive their sin and heal their land."* (2 Chronicles 7:14)

What does prayer for national revival look like today?

We held two-day prayer workshops in three different cities in India, with Serve India, the Council of Reformed Churches in India, and with the West Delhi Pastors Association. At the heart of our time together, we broke people into groups of seven and took time to look at the Lord's Prayer. Each person was assigned one of the seven parts of this prayer and instructed to discern the kingdom purpose behind the petition. The interaction was energetic, as these leaders realized that the Lord's Prayer is Jesus' guide and framework for all of his kingdom purposes. For example, "Your will be done," implies not only that we pray to love and submit to the will of the Father, but also that we seek to carry out his will by doing justice and mercy. In India, this meant praying about how to serve widows and orphans, praying against the caste system, and resolving to treat everyone with dignity.

For each part of the prayer, a different person shared their insights and then the whole group prayed through the prayer. The volume increased with fervent intensity as the group prayed through the prayer.

In Visakhapatnam, when we came near the end of our two days together, we circled around the large room to pray for the church of India and for the nation. First we faced one another, lifted our hands, and with one voice and one heart, prayed for one another and the church. As the Spirit deepened, the prayer increased in joyous unity. Children playing outside came in to see what was happening, and they too lifted their hands to join in.

After the prayer subsided it was time for chai tea. After tea, once again we circled the room. This time, hands raised, we faced outward and began to pray for India. I coached, "Wherever you are facing, pray for that region and its cities." With one voice, the assembly raised a cry to God for the land of India. Longing and hope were written on their faces as these people prayed for God to heal their land, forgive their sins, bring salvation to many, compel leaders to fear God, and protect the poor from oppression. One of the bishops raised a beautiful, sonorous voice in a well-known song for the church and the nation. The worship team joined in. Hands raised and hearts lifted, we sang and prayed with a single voice. Some kneeled, and others swayed with the music, united in full-throated song and full spectrum of emotions. I believe we were all thinking the same thing, "This is kingdom prayer. This is what you made us for, Lord."

An Example from History:
THE WELSH REVIVAL (1904)

Prayer revivals happen today. When we unite in repentant prayer for a city or nation, confessing our own wickedness and the sin of the land, we are promised great joy. Humble, repentant prayer still revives nations.

Just over a century ago, beginning in 1904, Wales experienced the last national religious revival, a revival that brought in more than 100,000 new converts according to the estimates of the time, and a movement that quickly spread to the four corners of the world. Yet that great movement of the

Spirit had very small beginnings that didn't always involve the great preachers of the day—erudite and educated as they were—but instead included, for instance, a young teenager from New Quay, Cardigan. Florrie Evans was in a youth meeting in February 1904, when she declared publicly that she loved the Lord Jesus with all her heart. With these words, the Spirit seemed to fall upon the gathering and quickly spread to other young people in the Cardiganshire area.

What was common throughout the revival was heart-rending repentance. Evan Roberts, a college student, was God's instrument to light the fire. In the middle of the night, for three months, he prayed for revival. While praying, he heard God's promise that many thousands would be saved. One Sunday evening he was permitted to preach a sermon to a small group. Roberts called his hearers to repentance and consecration. The outline of this message became the "four points of the revival:" first, confess all known sin; second, put aside all doubtful habits; third, promptly obey the Holy Spirit; fourth, make Christ known publicly. At the meeting, the Spirit did indeed come down. Roberts himself was overcome with awe, as people started yelling, "No more, Lord Jesus, or I die." Others cried for mercy, wept, sang, and praised God; this, together with "the sight of many who had fainted or lay prostrate on the ground in an agony of conviction," was "as unbelievable as it was unprecedented." Every night God would rouse others out of their sleep, convict them of sin and save their souls. And indeed, there were reports of people climbing out of their beds in the middle of the night, searching out a prayer meeting and crying out for the Lord Jesus to save them.

From that first meeting and that college student, word spread throughout Wales and so did the awakening. Church historian J. Edwin Orr reported that within three months 100,000 converts had been added to the churches of Wales. Alcoholism dropped by fifty percent. Crime plummeted so much that some judges were presented with white gloves, meaning there were no crimes to try. There was even a work slowdown in the coal mines because so many workers became converted and ceased using profanity.[2]

The Welsh Revival was the farthest-reaching movement of the general awakening, for it affected the whole of the evangelical cause in India, Korea, and China, renewed revival in Japan and South Africa, and sent a wave of awakening over Africa, Latin America, and the South Seas. Orr observed: "The early twentieth century Evangelical Awakening was a worldwide movement. It did not begin with the phenomenal Welsh Revival of 1904-05. Rather its sources were in the springs of little prayer meetings which seemed to arise spontaneously all over the world, combining into streams of expectation which became a river of blessing in which the Welsh Revival became the greatest cataract."

---

2 "The horses are terribly puzzled. A manager said to me: 'The haulers are some of the very lowest. They have driven the horses by obscenity and kicks. Now they can hardly persuade the horses to start working because there is no obscenity and no kicks." G. Campbell Morgan, Arthur Goodrich, William T. Stead, Evan Roberts. *The Welsh Revival & The Story of the Welsh Revival: As Told by Eyewitnesses.* (Lawton, OK: Trumpet Press, 2015).

KINGDOM-COME PRAYER TODAY

If revival starts with earnest, united, repentant prayer—ask yourself and discuss with others the following questions:

1. In three of the revivals studied, the enemy army is defeated by God, without human agency. What are the lessons in this for our times?

2. How bad are things today? Does this assessment of present evil and call to repentance ring true or is it overblown? How can we tell?

3. How much of our prayers are cries of repentance? How could we begin to incorporate this into our prayers?

4. In what ways can we gather together to pray for our nation and confess our personal and national sins to God?

5. For a practical and simple exercise on praying for the heart of your nation, see Appendix C.

CHAPTER 9

How Idols Are Removed Through Kingdom Prayer

Kingdom Prayer Discerns and Expels Prevailing Idolatry

In the Old Testament, as surveyed in the previous chapter, when it comes to idols it is a matter of "search and destroy." Righteous kings and devout people not only avoid the idols of the land, they do not rest until they are removed and destroyed. The death grip of idols breaks through humble, repentant prayer—and nothing else! Once the death grip is broken, the idols are ground to powder, and people return to the life-giving joy of prayer, worship, fellowship, and justice. Idols are rendered obsolete and worthy only of contempt:

> Then you will defile your carved idols overlaid with silver and your gold-plated metal images. You will scatter them as unclean things. You will say to them, "Be gone!" (Isaiah 30:22)

In one sense the whole Christian life is a battle with idols, for it is a battle for our hearts, minds, and imaginations. At its most basic level, an idol is any object, image, person, or idea that usurps God as the primary object of our devotion. In this chapter, we begin with the assumption that all people are religious, in the sense that everyone makes images and fixate on ideals that satisfy their own needs and aspirations. Even if someone is secular in the sense that they disavow any faith in God or gods, they cannot help but attach their innate capacity for worship onto something or someone. Whatever becomes the supreme object of their hearts' devotion is their god.

Mammon in Malaysia

In most ancient cities the city center was reserved for the temples and objects of worship, while the surrounding countryside housed shrines devoted to lesser gods. Worshipers would enter these shrines in service to their idols with rituals of worship and devotion, such as the offering of sacrifices, burning of incense, the speaking of prayers, paying of dues, and practicing of rites and rituals. In ancient times, temple prostitution and orgies were often part of the ceremony, especially when the god or goddess represented forces of fertility.

To seek out the idols of our cultures today, we need only pay a visit to the heart of a major city. It is here we find the objects of worship on full display. In traditional religious cultures in the East, for example, you can find a massive temple dedicated to Buddha at the center of Thailand's Chiang Mai.

Or consider Malaysia's capital city, Kuala Lumpur. Downtown, in the heart of this city, lies not a mosque or temple but massive twin towers of finance and retail. Though its people are very religious—sixty-one percent of Malaysians practice Islam, nineteen percent are Buddhists, nine percent Christians, and six percent Hindu—there are no temples where we might expect to find them. Instead, the Petronas Twin Towers, for many years the tallest skyscrapers in the world, stand more than eighty stories high and house the financial, technological, and business offices that power a global economy. It takes little imagination to deduce the idolatries fed by these engines of industry.

What captures our attention, however, is something else. Centered between the two towers, in the innermost chambers of this city, is a massive shopping mall filled with inviting, sexualized images of affluence and beauty. In its center is a public court, circled by floors of shoppers. Cathedral-like, a glass tower rises above it.

Location matters, and in most modern cities, like the ancient cities before them, the culture's temple resides in the center. The innermost chambers of the temple house the sanctum sanctorum where the chief idol resides. As we gather, like thousands of Malaysians, at the air-conditioned, glittering shopping center inside the Petronas Towers, we realize we have stumbled upon a place of worship.

The modern mall as today's temple

We pause to pray in front of the impressive towers. We have come to admire the stunning architectural wonder, as well as to understand the aspirations of the people of Kuala Lumpur. We assume that a view from the top of the Petronas Towers will give us a clue, but it turns out that much of our mission will be accomplished by surveying the city from ground level.

With more than a half hour until our scheduled trip to the tower's sky-bridge observation deck, we head down a set of stairs into the mall. Here we find people of many faiths and nationalities calmly milling about, sharing a collective experience of accessing global retailers—Victoria's Secret, Hugo Boss, TAG Heuer, among others—and anticipating the status inferred upon them as purchasers of global name-brand prestige. Floor to ceiling, glittering images of beautiful men and women, unstained by the hardships of life, exude eternal youth and beauty. These images' searching gaze, slightly parted lips, and artfully positioned limbs are charged with seductive sexual energy and promiscuous availability. Perfectly proportioned mannequins and exquisitely designed display cases resemble their own brand of graven images.

They are not unlike the carvings of gods, ample-bodied and suggestively postured, found at any Hindu temple. Their eyes invite you into their world, suggesting that "This can be yours! Yes, it costs, but how satisfying to walk among the glorious icons of our culture!" Their bodily presence, in the form of mannequin and marketing, call for worship of eternal youth, bodily perfection, physical beauty, earthly affluence, and celebrity fame.

Our experience of this visual extravaganza incites many questions: What does all this glamour—the shiny steel, architectural achievement, and flawless images—signify? What does it say about the heart of Kuala Lumpur (and the hearts of most modern cities with similar places of worship)? How did a mall come to be located at the heart and center of a religious city and who gave permission? While we might assume that something seemingly innocuous as a shopping mall poses no threat to the mosques and churches of the city, its strategic location and remarkable structure represent much more than a mere convenient shopping hub.

Materialism produces material images. The images of an electronic culture are powerful and seductive. They shine with beauty and entice us with a legion of unspoken promises. The reality is that the world's shiny screens and alluring images have already captured the hearts of mankind—not only secularists, but also pious Muslims, Hindus, Buddhists, and Christians. A splendid mall, along with its man made images, is permitted to occupy the center of the city because it has already proven stronger than the power of other gods. Not that the other gods have been utterly eliminated. The cohabitation of secular idols and images alongside the religions of the world demonstrates syncretism and accommodation. The promise is made: "You can keep your gods, just give us your heart."

Juxtaposing this scene at Petronas Towers with my recent experiences in India, I realize that the feelings of discomfort I experience in entering the mall are not dissimilar to those I had when visiting a temple in India. Devout Hindus visit a temple to secure favor and a better life. They may have selfish or even sinister motives in wanting to secure favors from the deity. The same could be said of most nominally religious people: Whether through ritual or prayer, what they seek is celestial favors in the form of status, sex, wealth, or power. This is exactly what a mall-as-temple promises with all its images of eternal youth, sexual beauty, and attainable affluence: Drink deep of this well. Buy in. All you need is new clothes, better cosmetics, and the latest technology, and then your dreams will come true. Everything you desire can be yours.

The power of Mammon

Secular materialism breeds material gods, whether in the form of shiny images or technological prowess. One might argue, "Cmon, these are just pictures of good looking people. They have no religious content or meaning. How can you call them idols?" The Bible says otherwise. Images of the ancient gods were just inert wood, metal, and stone. Similarly, idols on mall display or computer screen are lifeless, no matter how colorful and realistic they are. They have no real existence apart from the view of those devoted to them. Behold, you are nothing, and your work is less than nothing (Isaiah 41:24). Idolatry is in the eye of the beholder.

It is a mistake to underestimate materialism. In Milton's Paradise Lost, Mammon is one of the few gods to rival Satan in might and magnificence. A glimmering and sanitized mall presents the perfect place for Mammon to hide out. John Bunyan, in his allegorical work The Pilgrim's Progress, depicts such a place as Vanity Fair:

> Then I saw in my dream, that when they were got out of the wilderness, they presently saw a town before them, and the name of that town is Vanity; and at the town there is a fair

kept, called Vanity Fair. It is kept all the year long. It beareth
the name of Vanity Fair, because the town where it is kept
is lighter than vanity, and also because all that is there sold,
or that cometh thither, is vanity; as is the saying of the wise,
"All that cometh is vanity."[1]

As Bunyan points out, "the way to the Celestial City
lies just through this town, where this lusty fair is kept."[2]
Moreover, Bunyan notes that the pilgrim believers become
martyrs when they decry the idolatry of Vanity Fair's
commerce, lusts, and indulgences.

A binary, incestuous relationship exists between commerce
and idolatry. Consider the many warnings Jesus gave his disciples
about the powerful seduction of wealth and affluence[3] Consider
also Paul's confrontation with the Ephesian merchants and idol
craftsmen. When the gospel was preached in Ephesus, former
idol worshipers confessed faith in Christ, renounced their
idolatry, and destroyed their idolatrous images and books in a
massive bonfire (Acts 18:18-20). This public affirmation of Christ
infuriated the guild of craftsmen, not just for religious reasons,
but because of potential financial ruin:

> *About that time there arose no little disturbance concerning*
> *the Way. For a man named Demetrius, a silversmith, who*
> *made silver shrines of Artemis, brought no little business to the*
> *craftsmen. These he gathered together, with the workmen in*
> *similar trades, and said, "Men, you know that from this business*
> *we have our wealth. And you see and hear that not only in*
> *Ephesus but in almost all of Asia this Paul has persuaded and*
> *turned away a great many people, saying that gods made with*
> *hands are not gods. And there is danger not only that this trade*

---

1   John Bunyan, *The Pilgrim's Progress* (London: High Holborn,
1837), 151.
2   Ibid., 152-153.
3   Half of Jesus' parables (sixteen out of thirty-eight, to be exact)
warned about the lure and destructiveness of riches. Moreover, it is indeed
sobering that Jesus called out those who hated him and who would mas-
termind his crucifixion as "lovers of money."

of ours may come into disrepute but also that the temple of the
great goddess Artemis may be counted as nothing, and that she
may even be deposed from her magnificence, she whom all Asia
and the world worship." (Acts 19:23-27)

The era of man

This secular age is a new thing to the world. While formerly
many cultures produced idols that resembled a human likeness,
these idols did not represent man, they represented the gods.
But now, for the first time, man is forming images of himself.
This world was once believed to be the domain of God—his
creation. Now, the very idea of creation is vigorously dismissed.
Everything on earth is believed to have evolved on its own. The
world that was once owned by God we now claim for ourselves.
In a secular culture, there is no need for images or words about
God. In fact, to seriously intrude faith in God desecrates the
modern enterprise. Just as there is a sense of trespass when a
non-Hindu enters a Hindu temple, so too does mention of God
as Creator and Sovereign trespass on the inner sanctuary of
man's modern temples.

Men and women today still produce images of what they
worship. The fact that most of our representations are of man
and his enterprises indicate that man's idol today is man himself.
This has become the age of man, Where man exalts himself
above every object of worship (1 Thessalonians 2:3-4). Whatever
things capture the dreams and hopes of a people are the supreme
objects of their heart's affections. Whatever we look to for
deliverance in times of trouble is our idol. Even if one is secular,
he cannot help but pour his religious affections, hopes, and
longings into something or someone. John Calvin said it well:
The heart of man is a ceaseless idol factory.

Understanding modern idolatry

The second of the Ten Commandments forbids making
graven images. Graven images are merely objects and pictures
made by men. They become an idol when they demand our

attention and when we attach our hearts' affections and hopes
to them. If any object or image serves the same purpose as
an idol—it is, in fact, an idol. As in the Malaysian mall, the
proliferation of man made images cannot but capture our hearts
and imaginations. In time, these images take over, and we can
become irretrievably attached, even addicted, to what they
represent. Images become idols.

We recall a striking picture of the power of images at the
Petronas Mall. We had ascended a few floors to upper levels.
Looking down, we see perhaps forty or fifty people of every faith
and nation, taking it all in. They are milling about the common
space, simply absorbing the ambiance- some are seated on
benches in the area encircling the ground level. At that particular
moment, we notice that virtually everyone one within our view
is gazing intently at their cell phone. (Although, admittedly, one
couple shared a screen.)

Computers and mobile technology provide an infinite variety
of man made "graven images." Take, for example, the smartphone
with all its technological wonder—interactive applications,
communications, entertainment, games, and social media. It
calls out to us repeatedly, and we hasten to reply. We eagerly
await the next notification. We check our phones constantly to
stay connected or to fill downtime. We pay careful attention to
its diminishing battery power, lest we are left unconnected. It
takes scant argument to prove we have become attached, even
addicted, to our smartphones and the images they provide.

Underlying the expression of the smartphone lies our
culture's greatest idol, the chief god of our secular pantheon—
technology itself. Our ability to manipulate the environment,
alter our genes, provide unlimited comfort, and even stave off
death, allows us to imagine that we are now the sole masters
of our world and can reconfigure our own destiny. We have no
need of God. We were once content to be tenants of the vineyard
owned by another Lord, but the time has come for us to expel

the Owner and claim the vineyard for ourselves: But when the tenants saw the son, they said to themselves, "This is the heir. Come, let us kill him and have his inheritance." (Matthew 21:33-41) Dissatisfied with God's rule, we resolve to make an new world on our own.

The empty promises of idols

Idols are vain things, in the sense that they are devoid of life and unable to fulfill their ultimate promise:

Tell us what is to come hereafter, that we may know that you are gods; do good, or do harm, that we may be dismayed and terrified. Behold, you are nothing, and your work is less than nothing; an abomination is he who chooses you. (Isaiah 41:23-24)

Idols lead us to an empty and vain existence. Social media and electronic communication promise a clean and shiny world, but this world is sterile, empty of deep, personal, and meaningful relationships. In fact, we now know that the proliferation of information and connectivity has failed its inherent promise— what was meant to foster better relationships and flourishing humanity has failed to deliver, and we are far more fractured in our relationships and civility than ever before!

We imagine that our idols serve us; instead, we serve our idols. We become slaves to the man made images we create. Entertainment, pornography, video games, and social media capture not only our eyes but our hearts as well, eviscerating us of noble thought, meaningful conversation, and dignifying work. When we place our inner hopes and affections on idols, our souls are diminished, and we become like the idols we worship:

Our God is in the heavens; he does all that he pleases.
Their idols are silver and gold, the work of human hands.
They have mouths, but do not speak; eyes, but do not see.
They have ears, but do not hear; noses, but do not smell.
They have hands, but do not feel; feet, but do not walk; and they do not make a sound in their throat. Those who make them become like them, so do all who trust in them. (Psalm 115:4-8)

Like our lifeless idols, we end up dead in heart and mind, empty in soul and thought. We become programmed to the operations of the media objects we are attached to and end up living a futile, repetitious existence, feeding on the empty images we trust in:

> *Because you were absent, the whole world seemed to me tiny and ridiculous, and the destiny of man stupid and cruel.*
>
> *A world that was once Christian seems to be in the process of being emptied from within. It first loses God, then the son of God, then everything divine... It is often the surface that is the last thing to collapse.*[4]

Dismantling idols

In the Old Testament idolatry is the presenting sin from which other sins flow. Idolatry is the greatest sin, because loving God is the highest righteousness: The first and greatest commandment is "Love the Lord your God with all your heart mind and soul." (Matthew 22:37-38) While one might suppose that our treatment of others presents the highest good and greatest obligation, it is our treatment of God is the highest duty and our greatest privilege. God's Law, as listed in the Ten Commandments, reveal a distinct order: the first four commandments describes our duty to God, the last six such that being kind to one's neighbor is of no avail if someone is hateful or indifferent toward God. This is why God reserves his greatest indignation and most severe punishments for idolaters.

The Old Testament also reveals how the bondage of idols is broken—through humble and repentant prayer! Only then can kings and people identify and destroy the idols, leading to newfound joy, worship, fellowship, and justice. Idols are rendered obsolete and worthy of contempt:

---

4   Madeleine Delbrêl, *We, the Ordinary People of the Streets* (Grand Rapids, Mich: W.B. Eerdmans, 2000).

Then you will defile your carved idols overlaid with silver and your gold-plated metal images. You will scatter them as unclean things. You will say to them, "Be gone!" (Isaiah 30:22)

People who don't know God admit that it is impossible to turn off, restrain, or defeat the power of online media in its various forms. They surrender: "We have lost the battle." Shiny little screens offering endless self-entertainment have won the day. Meaningful dialogue and neighborliness have been exchanged for the self-gratification easily accessed on our media devices.

What is distressing is not so much the proliferation of technology or the succumbing of the culture to its power, but rather how easily Christian believers have given up the fight. We have surrendered the field to what we perceive to be an irresistible army of idols. With condescending glances and dismissive phrases, we refuse to believe the idols of today can be forsaken and destroyed. For this attitude and these words of resignation, God has strong words:

Your words have been hard against me, says the Lord. But you say, "How have we spoken against you?" You have said, "It is vain to serve God. What is the profit of our keeping his charge or of walking as in mourning before the Lord of hosts?" (Malachi 3:13-14)

It is understandable if we give up on our culture or even on ourselves. What is treasonous is giving in to unbelief that God can deliver us from the power of modern idols. What are we saying about God when we surrender to these graven images? More to the point, what are we saying about Jesus and about the power of his resurrection when we wave the white flag and give into a culture restless with greed? To make peace with the world and its idols invites strong rebuke:

In that day the Lord God of hosts called for weeping and mourning, for baldness and wearing sackcloth; and behold, joy and gladness, killing oxen and slaughtering sheep, eating flesh and drinking wine. "Let us eat and drink, for tomorrow we die."

> *The Lord of hosts has revealed himself in my ears: "Surely this iniquity will not be atoned for you until you die," says the Lord God of hosts.* (Isaiah 22:12-14)

This passage is a powerful call to repent of our unbelief. To give up on oneself is understandable. To give up on God is unforgivable.

Find Christ, find freedom

Contrary to the naysayers, it is not at all impossible to dismantle the idols of today. Many thousands have found a way to "fight the good fight of the faith" over the enticement of malls and attachment to smart phones and an idolatrous trust of technology. Through consistent prayer we discern today's idols and their power over us. Through kingdom prayer we pray for God's will to be done on earth as it is in heaven. Through disruptive prayer we plead for faith to believe the power of God's Spirit at work in us and in our world. Christ has not given up his throne, and prayer has not lost its power!

Find Christ, and you find freedom. Revel in the worship of the all-powerful King, and you will discover the mall to be a cheap substitute for real treasures. Once the King reigns in your affections, the idols will lose their power over you; you can walk through an image-laden mall unmoved by the allure of the idols being offered. Instead, your affections will focus on the souls of fellow shoppers, the justice of minimum-wage workers, the flourishing of local businesses, the prevention of harm from advertising's exploitation, and the protection of your community's most vulnerable citizens.

Discover God's friendship in prayer, and you will learn to despise self-obsessed trivialities and to forego self-entertainment. You can begin to give your moments and hours back to God and others who deserve it. Or do you not know that your body is a temple of the Holy Spirit within you, whom you have from God? You are not your own, for you were bought with a price. So glorify God in your body. (1 Corinthians 6:19-20) You will be able to turn off news notifications and unplug whenever you judge it helpful. You will have the discipline and power to make the technology serve you, rather than you serving it.

A way to destroy the power of idols

As we have seen in the Old Testament, the power of humble and repentant prayer is the way to break the stranglehold of idols. The idols of the nations surrounding Israel seemed indomitable. Yet, in response to the earnest, united, repentant prayer, God destroyed the idols in a moment. He reinstated the joy and rest that results from his righteous reign.

So where do we begin? The good news is that it's not complicated or arduous. We make great progress loosening the grip of idols when we simply re-engage in prayer and meaningful conversation. In fact, this is the first and indispensable antidote for breaking the back of technological idols. All idols and addictions are empty substitutes for a rich relationship with God and with others. As we rediscover the joy of prayer and the richness of conversation, we expose the emptiness of virtual communication. The adventure of following God, the soul-filling joy of friendship with fellow believers, and the challenges and hopes contained within our conversations will render our idols as unworthy. As we pray, God promises deliverance:

> For a people shall dwell in Zion, in Jerusalem; you shall weep no more. He will surely be gracious to you at the sound of your cry. As soon as he hears it, he answers you. And though the Lord give you the bread of adversity and the water of affliction, yet your Teacher will not hide himself anymore, but your eyes shall see your Teacher. And your ears shall hear a word behind you, saying, "This is the way, walk in it," when you turn to the right or when you turn to the left. Then you will defile your carved idols overlaid with silver and your gold-plated metal images. You will scatter them as unclean things. You will say to them, "Be gone!" (Isaiah 30:19-22)

Enjoy the feast of prayer communion. Get to know one another in prayer (the best way to get to know each other). Early Christians met together every day and were "devoted to prayer." They reaped a harvest of communion and a harvest of growth in evangelism:

> *And they devoted themselves to the apostles' teaching and the fellowship, to the breaking of bread and the prayers... And all who believed were together and had all things in common... And day by day, attending the temple together and breaking bread in their homes, they received their food with glad and generous hearts, praising God and having favor with all the people. And the Lord added to their number day by day those who were being saved.* (Acts 2:42ff)

As you mature in a prayer friendship with Jesus and his children, you will grow in love for eternal things. You will begin living in awe of God's power and majesty, relishing community with fellow believers, friends and neighbors, and enjoy a deepening wonder at the marvels of creation. This is a joy that cannot be taken away.

KINGDOM-COME PRAYER TODAY

1. Looking at the culture around you, what are the idols and images that capture people's imaginations, dreams, and true affections? What do people look to for deliverance in times of need or trouble?

2. In prayerful soul search ask yourself, "Where have I resigned myself to the culture and its idols?" "In what areas do I need to experience freedom from the images and instruments of idolatry in my life?" Repent where you have grieved the Holy Spirit through your unbelief

3. Prayerfully measure your digital usage and dependence on technology. Confess, in specific ways, wherever you have been taken captive in thoughts and habits. In reliance upon our spiritual-battle assets of prayer and power, resolve to consecrate yourself to a holy use of digital technology. Prepare to enter the fray as a faithful soldier of Christ.

CHAPTER IO

How Exiles Are Sustained Through Regenerating Prayer

How Prayer Sustains Kingdom Advance During Captivity

Throughout biblical history, Israel was unable to separate herself from surrounding cultures and became captivated by the idolatry and power of surrounding populations. To set his people free, God sent them into captivity.

His strategy might seem strange. Israel forsakes God's law and becomes an idolatrous nation—so God sends them to a city filled with idols. Israel is enamored with the world's power and prosperity—so God sends them to the most prosperous city the world has ever known. Babylon was called "the City of Gold" (Isaiah 14:5), comparable to today's Hong Kong, London, Paris, New York City, or a combination of them all!

It was strange therapy—but it worked! After returning from seventy years of captivity, the nation never worships idols again. God raises up leaders who champion Israel's full break with any and all forms of idolatry. When King Nebuchadnezzar erects a massive idol and commands people to worship it, three heroes defy the king and receive swift and horrifying retribution:

Shadrach, Meshach, and Abednego answered and said to the king,

> *O Nebuchadnezzar, we have no need to answer you in this matter. If this be so, our God whom we serve is able to deliver us from the burning fiery furnace, and he will deliver us out of your hand, O king. But if not, be it known to you, O king, that we will not serve your gods or worship the golden image that you have set up.* (Daniel 3:16-18)

We know the rest of the story. While the furnace heat ratchets up to supernova temperatures, "one like a son of man" joins them in the ordeal—and not a hair on their heads is singed. Not only so, but King Nebuchadnezzar recognizes his folly, reverses course, and requires his subjects to acknowledge the God of heaven.

As for Israel's fascination with the power and prestige of surrounding cultures, the Jewish people cultivate an extensive set of boundaries during their exile, in order to maintain ethnic and religious separation from all Gentile nations. By the time Christ arrived on the scene, they had gone too far in their boundary setting to the extent of excluding God seekers from entering the temple.[1]

The exiles' life of prayer

During their captivity, the Jewish people were deported from the promised land and separated from the temple and its rituals. They were stripped of their cultural and religious heritage,

---

1   See Chapter 3 "The King's Passion for Prayer"

denied season-marking festivals and temple worship, in essence, reduced to the essentials of simple, pure worship of God. Their simplified worship included keeping the Sabbath, reading the Torah, singing the psalms, and saying of prayers. If we are to judge from the biblical narrative in Daniel and Esther, prayer becomes the chief exercise of faith. In rabbinical teaching and popular piety, prayer takes the place of temple sacrifices. While in exile, pious Jews would pray three times each day (see Daniel 6). This daily practice accompanied them for the following centuries, even down to the present day.

We can overlay the narrative of Israel's captivity on to today's cultural and religious milieu, and in so doing will observe many parallels. Like captive Judah, we are resident aliens in our cities. We are called "sojourners and exiles." (1 Peter 2:11) In our day, the church of Christ is in constant danger of religious, political, and social captivity. The "world" embodies a domineering cultural, political, and religious force. The powers of our age often oppose the people of God and reject Christ's commands and values. The chasm between the kingdoms of this world and the kingdom of God widens every day.

Christians possess no claim to a promised land or temple. Like exiled Israelites, our worship since the time of Jesus' resurrection has been reduced to the bare essentials; the people of God devote themselves to the apostles' teaching and fellowship, to the breaking of bread, and prayers. (Acts 2:42) Our faith connection with God and our experience of his glorious presence are a matter of Word and Spirit, enjoyed through prayer. As John Calvin wrote, "The chief work of the Holy Spirit is faith. The chief act of faith is prayer."

Prayer lessons for exiles

Prayer rises from suffering and adversity.

Seventy years of exile and suffering humble the people of Israel and give them a thirst for God. Like nothing else, suffering teaches God's people to pray.

A vital relationship with the living God is sustained through prayer.

Before the captivity, Israel had become attached to external, material "saviors." They not only worshiped idols, but they confused temple rituals with a living relationship with God. They confused the seen world with the unseen. God weans his people from externals by confining them to the Word and to prayer; by doing so, he leads his people into a more profound and unseen faith. *"I will sprinkle clean water on you, and you shall be clean from all your uncleanness, and from all your idols I will cleanse you. And I will give you a new heart, and a new spirit I will put within you."* (Ezekiel 36:25ff)

God taught the Jewish people that right worship involves our innermost affections. An inner fire of faith must fuel outward practices. Sacrifices and rituals will not awaken Israel to God's presence and power; only a mighty work of God's Spirit will accomplish this.

This lesson of the exile can be applied to us today. For believers, worship and prayer are never a matter of rituals and buildings. Our faith is fueled by unseen realities.

> *The hour is coming, and is now here, when the true worshipers will worship the Father in spirit and truth, for the Father is seeking such people to worship him. God is spirit, and those who worship him must worship in spirit and truth.* (John 4:23-24)

God protects his people from political and cultural captivity through prayer.

As illustrated by the prayer life of Daniel, God's exiled people are to take their marching orders from God and not from existing powers. As Daniel prays, he discerns God's will and plan (Daniel 2:17, 9:3, 10:2). Far from being shaped by the dictates of kings, the political rulers of that day, seek Daniel's counsel and wisdom. These world rulers learn that God's kingdom is a mighty kingdom and his dominion endures from generation to generation (Daniel 4:3). Daniel prays for the kingdom of his captors, yet he always prays in order that the kingdom of God might be revealed.

Perhaps one of the greatest dangers for God's people today is political captivity. As faith in God declines in our secular society, trust is transferred to governing powers. When God's people become infected by this view of the world, they begin to look to political leaders for protection. When we fix our hopes on political leaders to protect the church and to determine the destiny of nations, we have already been taken captive.

In contrast, a life of prayer demonstrates our ultimate assent and affirmation of God's sovereignty in all the affairs of men. As we pray, we look to his Word and call upon him to guard his people, guide the church, and rule the world.

Rather than conform to the powers that be, Christians pray. On God's command, we pray that rulers, leaders, and culture-shapers in the surrounding world might be blessed, in order that we might cultivate godly lives and effectively proclaim the gospel. Even as we pray for the existing order, we pray for a new order to be revealed:

> *First of all, then, I urge that supplications, prayers, intercessions, and thanksgivings be made for all people, for kings and all who are in high positions, that we may lead a peaceful and quiet life, godly and dignified in every way. This is good, and it is pleasing in the sight of God our Savior, who desires all people to be saved and to come to the knowledge of the truth.* (1 Timothy 2:1ff)

God rescues his people from her enemies.

Consider Daniel's supplications and intercessions—he is a one-man prayer revolution. Over the many years of his tenure, at critical junctures, Daniel cries out to God. Each time he prays, it signals a dramatic rescue of God's people. Step-by-step, Daniel's prayers advance the kingdom cause.

For example, when Daniel unites in prayer with his friends, he is ushered into the halls of power. Daniel prays for wisdom to interpret Nebuchadnezzar's dream; God answers his prayer and gives him the interpretation. The outcome forestalls the execution of the ruler's wise men, and Daniel becomes first among the king's counselors (Daniel 2). He continues as chief advisor to all three kings of the exile.

Later, Daniel is given wisdom to interpret another vision. When King Belshazzar arrogantly chooses to drink from the vessels of the temple, he literally sees the writing on the wall. As the king dissolves in terror, Daniel calls him to repent and tells him that Babylon's days of world domination are over.

Eventually, under the seceding Persian Empire, Daniel continues as the chief advisor to the new king. You can imagine how incumbent counselors felt about this. Envious conspirators plot Daniel's demise. He is ordered to pray to King Darius and no other god. Rather than submit, Daniel flings open his windows and prays three times a day; for this he is thrown to the lions. We know the rest: God hears Daniel's prayers from the lion pit, and he is miraculously delivered with not a scratch on him. Moreover, his conspirators are destroyed by the lions meant for Daniel's demise: And before they reached the bottom of the den, the lions overpowered them and broke all their bones in pieces (Daniel 6:25).

Some years later, while the Jewish people remain scattered throughout the empire, God uses an ordinary, young Jewish woman to rescue the nation and overthrow Israel's enemies. To save his people, God allows Esther to become King Xerxes' queen. The king's advisor Haman conspires genocide for God's people, like Pharoah and later Herod, who slaughtered the innocent children. Esther intercedes. Before daring to petition King Xerxes, she calls on God's people throughout the empire to fast and pray. God answers in a mighty way: He rescues the Jewish people and saves them from extinction. God turns the tide of history and reverses the king's pronouncement of doom as Haman and other enemies are destroyed.

When church or nation is in crisis, we can learn powerful lessons from Daniel and Esther. Our adversity is God's opportunity. When the forces of this world threaten, we need to fast and pray before we do anything else. When we unite to fast and pray, we strengthen one another in the sure confidence that Almighty God is on the throne and that he appoints and dismantles nations according to his sovereign pleasure. As we pray in the name and sacrificial mediation of Jesus, God will send his thunder and earthquakes to turn the tide of history (Revelation 8:1-5). Our hope is not in men. Our help is in the name of the Lord. Call upon me in the day of trouble; I will deliver you, and you shall glorify me (Psalm 50:15).

God's people bless their captors in prayer.

God is a missionary God, and he has a missionary purpose for sending Judah into Babylon. He tells his people, "be holy as I am holy," yet God also intends that they care for those who do not know him. His forever purpose is that Abraham's children bless all nations. And in your offspring shall all the nations of the earth be blessed (Genesis 22:18). Even in exile, God's call to pray for the nations abides (Isaiah 56:7).

Even while they are banished, God gives the exiles a prayer directive. He calls his people to pray for the city of her captors. Seek the welfare of the city where I have sent you and pray to the Lord on its behalf, for in its welfare you will be your welfare (Jeremiah 29:7). This promise-filled call to prayer pulses like a heartbeat throughout the years of exile.

God's exiles are his missionaries.

As our societies grow more hostile to the gospel, it is easy to "hide our light under a bushel." Apart from prayer, we grow fearful of the surrounding culture. We form enclaves of self-protection and become ingrown. Our prayers and energies are spent on self-preservation. Bold mission in a hostile world requires God's presence and power. Apart from united prayer for the advance of the gospel, the prevailing powers can easily overwhelm and drive us back into ourselves.

Aware of the blatant wickedness and increasing anti-Christian atmosphere today, we might balk at praying for our cities. The words of Jeremiah, however, direct us to a higher calling. If Israel of old was able to pray for the arrogant, idol-ridden city of Babylon, then surely we can intercede in prayer for Toronto, Vancouver, Calgary, New York, Los Angeles, and Chicago, or any other city in the world. We are called to bless our fellow citizens and seek their well-being, not only because God requires it, but also because serving and praying for a healthy city serves the good of God's people and the advancement of the gospel.

Complete restoration comes through repentant prayer.

God sends his people to Babylon with a promise of restoration.

> *For thus says the Lord: When seventy years are completed for Babylon, I will visit you, and I will fulfill to you my promise and bring you back to this place. For I know the plans I have for you, declares the Lord, plans for welfare and not for evil, to give you a future and a hope. Then you will call upon me and come and pray to me, and I will hear you. You will seek me and find me, when you seek me with all your heart.* (Jeremiah 29:10-13)

Daniel recalls Jeremiah's promise. He represents the nation in a repentant plea to forgive and restore this people to the promised land. Daniel consecrates himself to intercession: *"Then I turned my face to the Lord God, seeking him by prayer and pleas for mercy with fasting and sackcloth and ashes. I prayed to the Lord God and made confession...."* (Daniel 9:1-3)

A passionate and urgent prayer of repentance follows. It is a prayer for the ages: We have sinned and done wrong and acted wickedly...We have not listened...To us belongs open shame...We have not entreated the favor of the Lord our God...

Daniel's prayer culminates in a mighty plea: *"O Lord, forgive. O Lord pay attention and act. Delay not, for your own names' sake."* (Daniel 9:4-19)

God hears Daniel's prayer and restores Israel from her captivity.

Increasingly, believers today feel captive to the surrounding culture. Christians not only face a general disdain for their beliefs and practices, but leaders in government, education, and the courts legislate laws that are anti-biblical and entirely averse to the cause of Christ. A Christian response goes far beyond the ballot box. Like Daniel, we need to intercede and repent on behalf of the church and nation: If my people who are called by my name humble themselves, and pray and seek my face and turn from their wicked ways, then I will hear from heaven and will forgive their sin and heal their land (2 Chronicles 7:14).

We may not be "highly favored" and mighty in prayer like Daniel, but we too can intercede for the church and nation. Realizing how God used Daniel's prayers to restore and revive Israel, why would we not also unite in earnest and concerted prayer?

A life of an exile, a life of prayer

Like the exiles of Daniel's day, we have no promised land or holy city. We, too, are aliens and sojourners with no fixed address. Our promised land and true residence is in heaven (Hebrews 13:14). Our worship is not a matter of outward temple or rituals; rather, our life in this world is sustained by prayer and Scripture.

Yet, perhaps more than any other time in recent history, the events of exile and captivity apply to the church of our time. As "exile Christians," we are never at peace with the present world order. Like righteous Lot, we are greatly distressed by the sensual conduct of the wicked (2 Peter 2:7) and have made a decisive break with the world around us.

At the same time, like Daniel, Christians serve as a blessing to those around them. Wherever you turn in the needy parts of our country—the inner city, the First Nations (or Native American) reserves, among refugees and immigrants—you see God's people hard at work praying and serving those in need. The world will always complain about Christians, but woe to this world if Christians were to be removed!

While Christians serve, they pray, crying out night and day on behalf of the church and for the land of their exile. As they pray, believers have their hopes fixed on God. Burning jealousy for Christ's honor fills them with a broad generosity; out of a renewed heart they yearn and pray for the ingathering of many.

The conquering force of prayer over the powers of the city is proven again and again in Scripture and in history. As the church unites in earnest prayer, she remains true to her Lord. Moreover, like salt and leaven, she permeates the culture, politics, and religious life of her captors. The gates of our cities open in answer to prayers, and God's people enter in and bless their neighbors (Acts 12:10).

An Example from Today:
CUBAN CHRISTIANS (2017)

Cuban Christians are exiles in both biblical and practical ways. In Cuba, believers are not part of the political process. They are not included in civic discourse. The church is separate from the halls of power. Yet, the church has a vibrancy and love that is palpable. Cubans love to pray, and they love to serve those in need. Christians do not complain about the government; instead, they pray for the government. They do not hide from the surrounding city; rather, they step out and serve the people in countless ways. Many churches hold sports camps for children and youth. When hurricanes hit, they set up food stations. In Old Havana, Christians are the ones repairing the crumbling facades of their streets. They serve meals to the elderly and disabled. Where and when they can, they preach the gospel. Everyday believers are faithful in sharing the gospel, and the Cuban people are attracted to the church. The church has multiplied more than tenfold over the past twenty-five years. Although the church lies on the margins of society, it is a city within the city. It is a counter-cultural source of hope in a communist country.

When we were in Cuba holding three full days of prayer evangelism workshops in three different cities. In one city we divided into pairs and headed to Fraternity Park; each pair had between two and four prayer-evangelism conversations. In prayer and in conversation, the gospel was richly shared. All those who went out were eager to share their experience. One conversation was held with Brian, the owner of an amulet shop, who grew interested as we talked and prayed for him. Then we chatted with Isabel, a desperately lonely woman whose son was in prison in America. We gave her a gift, as it was her birthday, and prayed blessings upon her. Next, we talked with Ryan, who was eager to get a Bible. We have good hopes for his salvation.

Afterward, we gathered as a group under the shadow of the national legislature. In a large circle, we held hands, shared testimonies, sang songs, and prayed prayers for the country of Cuba. Nearby, a woman read tarot cards for a few pesos, and three of our team members peeled off to share the gospel with them. After an energetic discussion, the woman removed her magic beads and asked to receive a Bible.

KINGDOM-COME PRAYER TODAY

1. In what ways are believers today threatened by political, religious, and cultural captivity? Where have we compromised and failed to be separate from the surrounding culture,and compromised our calling?

2. How can we bless the city? In what ways can we intercede for her well-being and prosperity?

3. How can we serve our communities with acts of justice and mercy?

4. Ask God to open the gates of the city for the free expression of the good news.

CHAPTER II

How Church is Revived and City is Renewed Through Prayer

Prayer Brings a New Song to the Church and Rejoicing to the City

As we pray your kingdom come, we ask for the awakening of the church, as well as the flourishing of the city in which she dwells. *"But seek the welfare of the city, to which I send you into exile, for in its welfare you will find your welfare."* (Jeremiah 29:7) Revivals begin with the rapid multiplication of new believers and congregations. As these newborn converts infiltrate the culture as Christian salt and leaven, the blessings of the kingdom permeate the surrounding culture, bringing healing and renewal.

The Old Testament books of Ezra and Nehemiah contain the story of the return of Jewish people to rebuild the temple. The reading of these books reveal how prayer brings together revival in the church and healing of the city.

At critical junctures throughout these books, we find numerous individual and congregational prayers that call down the Spirit's power for this kingdom project. Once the temple and city walls are completed, the temple is filled with rejoicing, and the city joins the song:

> *The two choirs that gave thanks then took their places in the house of God. And on that day, they offered great sacrifices, rejoicing because God had given them great joy. The women and children also rejoiced. And the joy of Jerusalem was heard far away.* (Nehemiah 12:27-43)

This is revival in its fullness: a revived church and a renewed city.

Temple revival and city renewal take time.

Holistic kingdom advance is not short term. In these Old Testament accounts, it takes more than ninety years to arrive at

EVENT [CHRONOLOGY OF EZRA]	YEAR
Cyrus king of Persia captures Babylon	539 BC
First year of King Cyrus: issues proclamation freeing Jewish exiles to return	538–537
Jewish exiles, led by Sheshbazzar, return from Babylon to Jerusalem	537?
Altar rebuilt	537
Temple rebuilding begins	536
Adversaries oppose the rebuilding	536–530
Temple rebuilding ceases	530–520
Temple rebuilding resumes (2nd year of Darius)	520
Temple construction completed (6th year of Darius)	516
Ezra departs from Babylon to Jerusalem (arrives in 7th year of Artaxerxes)	458
Men of Judah and Benjamin assemble at Jerusalem	458
Officials conduct three-month investigation	458-457

Event [chronology of nehemiah]	Month/Day	Year
Hanani brings Nehemiah a report from Jerusalem (20th year of Artaxerxes I)		445–444 BC
Nehemia before King Artaxerxes	1	445
Nehemiah arrives to inspect Jerusalem walls		445
Wall is finished	6/25	445
People of Israel gather	7	445
People of Israel celebrate Feast of Booths	7/15–22	445
People of Israel fast and confess sins	7/24	445
Nehemiah returns to Jerusalem (32nd year of Artaxerxes I)		433–432

the noted celebration. Returning exiles lay the foundation of the temple in 537 BC; later generations complete the rebuilding of the city walls in 445 BC. In other words, it takes almost a century for the temple and city to come together.

We see a similar time span for the awakened church to permeate and transform English society after the Great Awakening. The revival started with an all-night prayer meeting in 1739 (see Chapter 7). Although the Spirit's power came upon the Methodists and sparked the revival through the preaching of George Whitefield within a matter of weeks, it took almost a century for the resulting "salt" to transform English society. The society-changing work of William Wilberforce and the Clapham Sect sprouted up a century later, culminating in the abolition of slavery in 1833.

There are lesser revivals before the great celebration of Nehemiah. After the temple foundations are set in place in 537 BC, a celebration is held: *"When the builders laid the foundation of the temple of the Lord...all the people gave a great shout of praise to the Lord."* (Ezra 3:11-14)

This modest beginning is short lived. The exiles cave under pressure from the surrounding foreigners, and construction of the temple halts. Both priests and people leave the city and drift back to their homes.

After ten years, the prophet Haggai wakes the people's conscience: *"Is it a time for you yourselves to be living in your paneled houses while this house remains a ruin?"* (Haggai 1:4)

Finally, twenty years after starting the project, the temple is rebuilt:

> *So the elders of the Jews continued to build and prosper under the preaching of Haggai the prophet and Zechariah, a descendant of Iddo. They finished building the temple according to the command of the God of Israel and the decrees of Cyrus, Darius and Artaxerxes, Kings of Persia.* (Ezra 6:15)

Temple service is restored, and the community marks the achievement: *"Then the people of Israel—the priests, the Levites and the rest of the exiles—celebrated the dedication of the house of God with joy."* (Ezra 6:16)

However, this revival also subsides, and there is a sixty-year gap in the narrative. Jerusalem enters into yet another period of religious and social decline. The people desert the temple service and abandon city precincts; the walls of the city remain in ruins.

In the west, we are in the early stages of church revival and urban renewal. Until the Lord grants a mighty awakening, we faithfully and patiently wait for the leaven to do its work. It is easy to grow weary as we pray and serve, as we consider the immensity of the task and the slow progress of change. Often, hearts will seem cold, and doors appear closed. I pray to be strengthened with all power, according to his glorious might, for all perseverance and endurance with joy (Colossians 1:11). I try be careful that I don't despise the day of small things (Zechariah 4:10).

Some questioned why David Livingstone hiked 29,000 arduous miles through jungles and deserts to explore and map Africa. Livingstone's stirring words explain: "Missionaries in the midst of heathenism seem like voices crying in the wilderness... future missionaries will see conversions follow every sermon. We prepare the way for them. May they not forget the pioneers who worked in the thick gloom with few rays to cheer, except such as flow from faith in God's promises! We work for a glorious future that we are not destined to see. We are only morning stars shining in the dark, but the glorious morn will break..."[1]

Most importantly, when the going gets tough, we are encouraged to fix our eyes on Jesus... who for the joy that was set before him endured the cross, despising the shame, and is seated at the right hand of the throne of God (Hebrews 12:2). When we pray with the eyes of faith, we see Jesus as he is now, and we participate in the victory of his death and the power of his ascension glory. In other words, we never pin our hopes or fix our gaze on external results for our labors. Looking to Jesus in prayer, we are confident he is working in and through us: I call out to God who fulfills his purpose for me (Psalm 52:7).

The fate of the church is always connected to the fate of the city.

One reason for this neglect of both temple and city is that the ongoing service of the temple depends on the safety provided by a strong and secure city. As long as the city walls lie in ruin, the temple remains unprotected. Clearly, the fate of the temple is tied to the fate of the city.

It is the same today. In many different ways, the fate of the church is tied to the fate of the cities we live in. It is hard for the church to flourish as long as the city is in decline. For example, in Canada, the church is weakened because, metaphorically, the walls of our cities are weak and the gates are broken. We have diced our neighborhoods with highways. We scatter our population with urban sprawl. Because we live, work, and play in different places, we have little time to invest in community life. City living becomes fragmented; its citizens are exhausted by the increasing demands of urban life.

Our fragmented and frenzied lifestyle works against the forming of strong social bonds and church fellowships.

---

1 W. Garden Blaikie, *The Personal Life of David Livingstone*, (Public Domain, 1880).

Urban renewal begins with repentance.

Returning to the biblical narrative, Ezra encounters a sad situation when he arrives in Jerusalem nearly sixty years later. The temple lies abandoned. The city walls are in ruins. Not only did the people neglect each other, but certain wealthy and propertied Jews enslaved those who could not pay their debts. Others had intermarried with Gentiles, further diluting their Jewish distinctiveness and disobeying God's law.

Ezra calls a fast for repentance. Out of his passionate prayer will arise a new awakening:

> I tore my garment and my cloak and pulled hair from my head and beard and sat appalled. Then all who trembled at the words of the God of Israel, because of the faithlessness of the returned exiles, gathered around me while I sat appalled until the evening sacrifice. And at the evening sacrifice I fell upon my knees and spread out my hands to the LORD my God, saying:

> "O my God, I am ashamed and blush to lift my face to you, my God, for our iniquities have risen higher than our heads, and our guilt has mounted up to the heavens....But now for a brief moment favor has been shown by the LORD our God...that our God may brighten our eyes and grant us a little reviving in our slavery." (Ezra 9:4ff)

God honors the fast, answers Ezra's prayer, and revives the hopes of the people.

However, this revival is also short-lived; fourteen years of inactivity follow, and once again we find that temple service is neglected and the city is abandoned.

God sends a city builder to unify temple and city.

Revival in its fullness does not happen until God sends a city-builder to Jerusalem. When Nehemiah hears that the walls of Jerusalem lie in ruins, he fasts and prays for four months, from Chislev (December) to Nissan (April). In deep shame and humiliation, Nehemiah confesses his own sin and the wickedness of his people. His majestic prayer echoes the words of King Solomon's prayers (2 Chronicles 6).

I sat down and wept and mourned for days, and I continued fasting and praying before the God of heaven. And I said, "O Lord God of heaven, the great and awesome God who keeps covenant and steadfast love with those who love him and keep his commandments, let your ear be attentive and your eyes open, to hear the prayer of your servant that I now pray before you day and night for the people of Israel your servants, confessing the sins of the people of Israel, which we have sinned against you. Even I and my father's house have sinned.... Remember the word that you commanded your servant, Moses, saying, 'If you are unfaithful, I will scatter you among the peoples, but if you return to me.... I will gather them and bring them to the place that I have chosen, to make my name dwell there.'...O Lord, let your ear be attentive to the prayer of your servant, and to the prayer of your servants who delight to fear your name, and give success to your servant today, and grant him mercy in the sight of this man. (Nehemiah 1:4-11)

Nehemiah's prayer bears fruit. King Artaxerxes intervenes for the returning exiles and sends Nehemiah to Jerusalem to rebuild the city walls.

Upon his arrival, before meeting with anyone, Nehemiah takes a prayer-walk. He circles the city to assess its broken walls. He wants to see things from God's perspective: *"I went out by night...and I inspected the walls of Jerusalem that were broken down and its gates that had been destroyed by fire.... Then I went up in the night by the valley and inspected the wall...."* (Nehemiah 2:13-14)

Nehemiah's prayer-walk leads to a prophetic call to action:

Then I said to them, "You see the trouble we are in, how Jerusalem lies in ruins with its gates burned. Come, let us build the wall of Jerusalem, that we may no longer suffer derision." And I told them of the hand of my God that had been upon me for good, and also of the words that the king had spoken to me. And they said, "Let us rise up and build." (Nehemiah 2:17-18)

God's people set to work and the walls are repaired in just fifty-two days.

Once the bronze gates of the city are hung in place, Jerusalem is able to provide safety for its inhabitants and protection for the temple. After ninety-three years of revival and decline, the temple and the city are finally in harmony.

It is time to celebrate! Priests, leaders, and people come together to keep the Feast of Booths:

> And all the assembly of those who had returned from the captivity made booths and lived in the booths, for from the days of Jeshua the son of Nun to that day the people of Israel had not done so. And there was very great rejoicing...." (Nehemiah 8:17-18)

The week concludes with a full day of Scripture reading and prayer led by Ezra. There is a heartfelt confession of sin, and a covenant is made with the intent to repopulate the city (Nehemiah 9:10-11).

This happy peace between temple and city leads to a thanksgiving celebration of cosmic proportions. Worshiping priests and festal choirs parade around the three-kilometer parapet that encircles the city. Filling out the grand assembly are forty thousand people who crowd the temple courts:

> At the dedication of the wall of Jerusalem, the Levites were sought out from where they lived and were brought to Jerusalem to joyfully celebrate the dedication with songs of thanksgiving and with the music of cymbals, harps, and lyres. The musicians also were brought together from the region around Jerusalem—from the villages...for the musicians had built villages for themselves around Jerusalem. I also assigned two large choirs to give thanks. One was to proceed on top of the wall to the right, toward the Dung Gate.... The second choir proceeded in the opposite direction.... At the Gate of the Guard they stopped. The two choirs that gave thanks then took their places in the house of God.... And on that day, they offered great sacrifices, rejoicing because God had given them great joy. The women and children also rejoiced. (Nehemiah 12:27-43)

The two choirs meet together atop the wall overlooking the temple. They form a congregation of five hundred worshipers. Men and women singers lift their songs until tears cover their faces. Two hundred priests and Levites blow the trumpet-like shophar. Others play musical instruments to praise God with all their might. The thousands of people filling the temple courts join in. They all sing the Great Hallel:

> *Praise the LORD! Praise the LORD, you his servants; praise the name of the LORD! Let the name of the LORD be praised, both now and forevermore! From the rising of the sun to the place where it sets, the name of the LORD is to be praised!"* (Psalm 113:1-5)

This is what the prophets, priests, kings, and people have been waiting for. At long last, the city and the sanctuary are in harmony. The renewed city protects the temple, while temple worship brings life to the city. The vision and promises of the prophets have come to pass. *"Build my temple so that I might be honored and be pleased in it."* (Haggai 1:8)

This has always been God's plan and promise: a city protecting the temple; a temple pulsing with the Spirit, bringing laughter and joy to the heart of the city.

This history of revival contains lessons for today.

We can make several applications to our present situation.

First, revival in its fullness requires time; short-term strategies for church revival and urban renewal are unrealistic and naive. Urban mission needs to be measured in decades, not years. There will be times of harvest and seasons of revival, but there will also be opposition, seen and unseen, both inside and outside the walls. Like leaven, the kingdom of God starts small and takes time, but eventually, everything is transformed.

Second, church and city often exist in tension. In our day the church suffers neglect, and the spiritual and moral walls of the city are in decay. I see violence and strife in the city. *"Day and night they go around it on its walls, and iniquity and trouble are within it; ruin is in its midst; oppression and fraud do not depart from its marketplace."* (Psalm 55:9-11) Foundations need to be rebuilt, and this always takes longer than the primary structure. Much groundwork will remain hidden and unheralded.

Third, as we unite in prayer, God will raise up leaders for the work. Consider the preceding history, in which God conscripted mighty kings—Cyrus, Darius, and Artaxerxes—to support the temple project. He sent prophets such as Haggai, Zechariah, and Malachi to encourage the building of the temple and to reignite dying embers of revival. God raised up godly leaders of courage—temple-builders like Zerubbabel, preachers like Ezra, and city-builders like Nehemiah. Time and again, the priests, the Levites, and the people offered themselves in holy array and service to God's kingdom purposes. As we unite to pray today, God will conscript rulers, send prophets, raise up builders, and enable workers for the rebuilding of his house. If we wholeheartedly give ourselves to prayer, we will witness the harmony God can bring upon the church and city.

Jesus is the one who brings harmony.

It is Christ who ultimately brings church and city together. The prophets, priests, and kings who rebuild the city and the temple in Jerusalem are a composite picture of Jesus—the final prophet, the perfect priest, and the everlasting king—who builds, cleanses and inhabits his temple. We heard him say, *"I will destroy this temple that is made with hands, and in three days I will build another, not made with hands."* (Mark 14:58)

At the same time, even now, Jesus is building an eternal and perfect city whose architect and builder is God (Hebrews 11:10). He is preparing the New Jerusalem, the perfect temple-city (see Revelation 21). Likewise, those who believe in Jesus embody a living, breathing temple-city as we await the eternal, unshakable kingdom to come:

You also, like living stones, are being built into a spiritual house to be a holy priesthood, offering spiritual sacrifices acceptable to God through Jesus Christ....But you are a chosen people, a royal priesthood, a holy nation, God's special possession, that you may declare the praises of him who called you out of darkness into his wonderful light. (1 Peter 2:9)

Christians are called to be church-builders and city-builders.

Our kingdom calling is to build the church and renew the city.

To build the church, we unite in prayer and beseech the Spirit's power. We become a house of prayer for the nations (Isaiah 56:7). We serve God's people with generous joy and gracious self-giving.

To build the city, we first acknowledge the biblical mandate to be city builders. We are called to dwell in the city, to pray for the city, to repair the city, and to fill the city with joy and justice:

If you spend yourselves in behalf of the hungry and satisfy the needs of the oppressed...then your light will rise in the darkness, and your night will become like the noonday. Your people will rebuild the ancient ruins and will raise up the age-old foundations; you will be called Repairer of Broken Walls, Restorer of Streets with Dwellings. (Isaiah 58:10, 12)

God provides the blueprint. It is up to us to build the showhome that reveals what, one day, the new neighborhood will be like.

In Canada today new churches are being established in the heart of many cities and on the campuses of many universities. Alpha Canada's outreach to youth is spreading to hundreds of high schools and they are reaching prisons across the country. Courageous Christians minister to new immigrants and serve in destitute neighborhoods.

Yet, for the most part, the church and the city seem removed from each other. Sunday churchgoing remains disconnected from city life. The church lies on the periphery. The sanctuary is separate from the city; it's as if someone has turned out the lights and locked the doors. While church attendance declines, the surrounding urban culture becomes increasingly cynical and gospel-resistant. God's people often seem strangely complacent and silent, migrating to private residences and living private lives. From self-protective enclaves, most believers do not take the time to pray for the church or the city.

Prophets and preachers like Haggai and Zechariah are needed to call us to repentance. We need for God to raise up temple-builders like Ezra and city-builders like Nehemiah.

We will know that our prayers are bearing fruit when the church is revived and the city is renewed. Those who pray the promises of God can rest in his timing and truth: No matter how long it takes, revival will come in response to prayer. It is not a matter of if; it is a matter of when.

We pray for the day when the city walls will be in place to protect the sanctuary. The outcome will be pure and joyous worship that glorifies God and fills the city!

We will know God has answered our prayers and blessed our labors when the walls of the city are in place and the gates are open to those who seek to know God—people from every nation can stream in and be taught his glorious way of salvation. The gates will close to observe Sabbath worship and to keep trade and commerce at bay.

Homes will be inhabited and streets filled with the joyous sounds of children at play. Community life will flourish; justice and truth will be the hallmarks of city life.

An Example From History: CUBA (1940-Present)

Reminiscent of Jerusalem's post-exilic period of decline is the recent history of Cuba. In the late 1950s not all Christians were opposed to Castro's communist revolution, yet after the communists came to power, the church was widely persecuted. Pastors and congregants went into hiding, and some were imprisoned. The gates of the country closed to the voices of its Christian citizens, as well as to foreign Christian missionaries.

Yet God has been raising up another city within the city. Since 1990 the church of Christ has rapidly grown within Cuba. Believers preach boldly, pray urgently, and worship vibrantly. In keeping with their love of culture and the arts, one congregation spends weeks repairing old buildings in the surrounding neighborhood. A young couple begins an outreach ministry to the arts community, hoping to establish a creative congregation in the city center. Recently, as police reported to one pastor, there was a forty percent decline in crime since that church's outreach began in the neighborhood. The seed has been sown, and the leaven is working.

One Christian group that had been poised to split, in the 1990s, over issues of liberty and legalism stayed together and now comprise two hundred churches and more than a thousand house churches. In recent years, its leaders have introduced gospel renewal and kingdom prayer; it has established five training centers and trained around eight thousand pastors!

The testimony of a Cuban church leader demonstrates how prayer unites church and city: "Cubans love art. Cuban artists paint the thoughts they are not free to express in words. Each week we host art evenings in the church so that local artists can gather to sip coffee, display and discuss their art." The pastor reports that eight house churches have been started and that thirty artists have come to faith in Christ in the first five years of this ministry. He tells us, "When we came to Hoguin, our launch team went to a hilltop overlooking the city and circled in prayer. We not only prayed to start new churches, we prayed kingdom prayers and asked God to help us reach and bless the whole city."

KINGDOM-COME PRAYER TODAY

1. Get to know your city or community at the ground level. Prayer-walking the community is a great way to see things from God's perspective. Like Nehemiah, circle the downtown of your city and survey the state of its "walls." Give thanks for churches and missions that are seeking to serve God and the community. Pray for centers of influence—media, arts, education, government, and industry.

2. Pray that God will give you his eyes to see and his heart to care. Seek to gain Christ's compassion and "harvest eyes" for your neighborhood (see Matthew 9:37-38).

3. Make your thanksgivings public. Don't confine your worship to Sunday mornings and your own prayer closet. Express thanks to God in everyday conversation.

Praying the Spirit's Vision

"Lord, Revive Your People and Heal Our Land"

The Bible narrative is the greatest of stories, told by God himself. Like all great stories, events coalesce in striking, unforgettable images. In particular, the prophets bring history and poetry together in illustrations and metaphors supplied by the Spirit. The life and flow of the coming kingdom are portrayed in majestic visions of hope.

We see prominent images of Holy Spirit revival from Isaiah, Zechariah, and Ezekiel, and the grand finale from Revelation. Prayer, temple, and city motifs repeat. From temple and city flow a river of salvation and healing, bringing the entire story to its glorious fulfillment.

Visions provide hope in times of defeat and captivity. As God's people study these depictions of the Spirit, they lift their eyes in prayer, and they anticipate a coming day of fulfillment. On the approaching horizon of their spiritual vision, rising like the morning sun, a "forever" day is coming when sanctuary and city will be one. In the midst of a troubled world, their prayer is filled with a holy longing. A day is coming when the nations will stream into the temple through the city gates. Ever deepening rivers of life emerge from the temple at the heart of the city, and bring healing to the entire land.

Sometimes we wonder if we are on our own as we labor and pray for church, city, and nation. Darkness can overtake our soul. A cynical voice within whispers, "No one cares, indifference is everywhere, the opposition is just too strong. You are praying and working in vain."

To help us through the darkness and give us fresh courage and hope, God gives us visions that cluster many of his promises. God's exceeding great and precious promises [are] like a light in a dark place until the day dawns and the morning star rises in your hearts (2 Peter 1:4,19). These visions are more than a prediction of the future, they are God's pledge and vow that he will soon bring to pass all that he promises—far above all that we can ask or think (Ephesians 3:20).

A multi-national vision for prayer

The first vision we consider is from Isaiah 56. When God opens Isaiah's eyes of faith, the prophet sees foreigners joyfully streaming into the temple to pray. The gates never close. These guests are invited and ushered in by God himself:

> *And the foreigners who join themselves to the Lord, to minister to him, to love the name of the Lord, and to be his servants, everyone who keeps the Sabbath and does not profane it, and holds fast my covenant—these I will bring to my holy mountain, and make them joyful in my house of prayer; their*

*burnt offerings and their sacrifices will be accepted on my altar;
for my house shall be called a house of prayer for all peoples.*
(Isaiah 56:7-9)

Newcomers are not segregated to an outer court. They are
not spectators; with all the sons and daughters of Abraham, they
are brought into joyful and ecstatic prayer fellowship with God.

As we pray into this vision today, several things happen.
We begin to take notice of the immigrants, refugees, and
international students who are filling our cities. Our hearts
are moved to prayer by their dislocation, their loneliness and
distress, and the challenges of raising children and finding
work in a strange, new land. As our hearts are stirred, our doors
open to show them love; the greatest gift we can offer our new
neighbor is hospitality. Often the best gift we can offer to people
of other cultures is to say a prayer for them, in their presence.
The word "hospitality"—philoxenos—literally means "loving the
stranger." Christians have always been rich in hospitality.

A vision of urban joy

The next prayer vision of the Spirit is from Isaiah 58, where
the prophet foretells the restoration of the city. At first, this city
is lying in rubble, in ruins to its very foundations. The process of
rebuilding begins with acts of mercy and justice:

*Is not this the fast that I choose: to loose the bonds of
wickedness, to undo the straps of the yoke, to let the oppressed go
free, and to break every yoke? Is it not to share your bread with
the hungry and bring the homeless poor into your house; when
you see the naked, to cover him, and not to hide yourself from
your own flesh?* (Isaiah 58:6,7)

God hears the cry of those who pour out their lives to clothe
and shelter others. He reveals himself to those who serve and
pray for the needy. Then, God sends those who pray to do this
work, giving them the unmerited honor of rebuilding the city
from the ground up:

*Then you shall call, and the Lord will answer; you shall cry, and
he will say, 'Here I am.'... And your ancient ruins shall be rebuilt;
you shall raise up the foundations of many generations; you
shall be called the repairer of the breach, the restorer of streets to
dwell in.* (Isaiah 58:9, 12)

As we pray this vision of hope for the city, it is already
coming to pass! We become what we pray, and God brings
to pass what we pray. As someone has said, "Christians are
building the show-home so everyone can see what the new
neighborhood will look like."

As we pray, God gives us the resolve to rebuild the city from
the ground up. God gives the strength to remove the rock and
rubble from the streets, and he gives the wisdom to re-lay the
foundations. God blesses us with perseverance as we pray and
labor to bring joy, safety and hope to the streets.

In many countries, Christians are rebuilding the streets of the
city. In India, for example, Serve India feeds, tutors, and cares for
thousands of orphans. We have seen it. Hope fills the bright eyes
of these children and laughter and joy rise from streets of play.

A city surrounded by prayer

In a third vision, God commands vigilant prayer for the city.
He sets forth his mandate in this striking image of watchmen
standing guard on the parapets of the holy city:

*On your walls, O Jerusalem, I have set watchmen; all the day and
all the night they shall never be silent. You who put the Lord in
remembrance, take no rest, and give him no rest until he establishes
Jerusalem and makes it a praise in the earth.* (Isaiah 62:6,7)

In every period of history, God appoints courageous prayer
warriors to guard the city. They man the ramparts. They walk the
walls. Those who pray for the city are ever vigilant and intent on
a single purpose. They pray without ceasing until God brings the
city and people of God to his promised destiny.

Every believer is called to be a prayer warrior. If we wonder
why there is so much corruption, violence, and desolation in our

cities today, we need look no further than here; the church has failed to guard and keep watch over the city. We have focused on private and personal concerns and left the walls of the city open to every vile and harmful influence. There is no greater need in the world today than for God to raise up a new generation of prayer warriors to guard our cities.

The Spirit's cleansing outpouring

In terse words, Zechariah's vision summarizes the entire history of the kingdom advance. An outpouring of Holy Spirit prayer initiates the coming of the kingdom. Preaching the message of Christ brings God's people to repentance and converts a multitude. As the tide rises, it sweeps away idols and lies.

> And I will pour out on the house of David and the inhabitants of Jerusalem a spirit of grace and pleas for mercy, so that, when they look on me, on him whom they have pierced, they shall mourn for him, as one mourns for an only child, and weep bitterly over him, as one weeps over a firstborn....On that day there shall be a fountain opened for the house of David and the inhabitants of Jerusalem, to cleanse them....And on that day, declares the Lord of hosts, I will cut off the names of the idols from the land, so that they shall be remembered no more. And also I will remove from the land the prophets and the spirit of uncleanness.... (Zechariah 12:10-13:3)

This vision contains a sequence and a priority.

First, this prophecy reveals that there is no use trying to change the city before God pours out a Spirit of prayer. The momentum of renewal will be stalled forever until God's people cry out in mourning and repentance.

Second, the headwaters are the Spirit's river of prayer; from this outpouring, the cleansing cataract of forgiveness will be released, and more and more converted to the King.

Third, only after these things happen will the floodtide of salvation overwhelm the idols and propaganda that permeate and corrupt the present order.

Zechariah's vision captures the sequence of prayer revival. In every great awakening in the biblical history, and in church history since, we see the order found in Zechariah 12:10-13:2 repeated. A spirit of prayer comes first in both sequence and priority. Repentance follows the Spirit's outpouring. Spiritual regeneration and forgiveness follow as more and more are saved. Finally, idols and false teachers drown in the river of justice and righteousness.

The vision of a river of prayer

When we get to the vision in Ezekiel 47, the prophet paints a picture of national renewal. An ever-deepening river flows from the temple and brings healing to the entire nation. We are invited to dive in, go deeper, and navigate its cascading life. We dare not stay on the shore.

> *Behold, water was issuing from below the threshold of the temple toward the east...trickling out on the south side. Going on eastward with a measuring line in his hand, the man measured a thousand cubits, and then led me through the water, and it was ankle-deep. Again he measured a thousand, and led me through the water, and it was knee-deep. Again he measured a thousand, and led me through the water, and it was waist-deep. Again he measured a thousand, and it was a river that I could not pass through. It was deep enough to swim in, a river that could not be passed through....*

> *Where the river goes the waters of the sea become fresh; so everything will live where the river goes. Fishermen will stand beside the sea...it will be a place for the spreading of nets.... And on the banks, on both sides of the river, there will grow all kinds of trees for food. Their leaves will not wither, nor their fruit fail, but they will bear fresh fruit every month, because the water for them flows from the sanctuary. Their fruit will be for food, and their leaves for healing.* (Ezekiel 47:1-12)

In the visible world, the river flows into and through the city. In this vision, the river flows from the city outward. It is an eternal spring that wells up from the temple within. (John 14:14) The altar it flows from is positioned at the exact center of the city.

Flowing outward from the altar, this stream deepens and broadens into a river. It begins as a mere trickle, but as it progresses it expands and strengthens because of the inexhaustible springs within.

The flow that swells from a trickle to a mighty river is a metaphor for the onward advance of God's kingdom. With unstoppable momentum, the stream pours through history, from generation to generation. As it spreads, its influence deepens, and eventually, the whole world will know its life-giving properties. It is the river of Spirit poured out upon all lands and all nations.

Step-by-step, we are invited into its depths, "Leave the shore. Step in up to your ankles and feel the flow. Go deeper and feel its power. Dive in and enjoy its healing." It is by prayer that we dive in. It is by prayer that we go deeper. It is by prayer that we learn to navigate its current and flow. Prayer Current ministry uses this vision of Ezekiel as the inspiration for our mission.

The heart-capturing finale

In the grand vision of Revelation 21, we come to the end and the fulfillment of the story. The storm has ended. The raging river returns to its steady course. As the forward movement of the kingdom subsides, it arrives at its everlasting destiny. All the streams and tributaries of the biblical narrative flow into this final vision of the new and eternal temple city.

"Come, I will show you the Bride, the wife of the Lamb." The angel carried me away in the Spirit to a great, high mountain, and showed me the holy city Jerusalem coming down out of heaven from God, having the glory of God, its radiance like a most rare jewel, like a jasper, clear as crystal. It had a great, high wall, with twelve gates, and at the gates twelve angels, and on the gates the names of the twelve tribes of the sons of Israel were inscribed—on the east three gates, on the north three gates, on the south three gates, and on the west three gates. And the wall of the city had twelve foundations, and on them were the twelve names of the twelve apostles of the Lamb.

And the one who spoke with me had a measuring rod of gold to measure the city and its gates and walls. The city lies foursquare, its length the same as its width. And he measured the city with his rod, 12,000 stadia. Its length and width and height are equal. He also measured its wall, 144 cubits by human measurement, which is also an angel's measurement.

To put things in perspective, the New Jerusalem is massive—a thousand times the size of Ezekiel's city—covering an area larger than India. The walls literally reach into the heavens—more than 2000 kilometers high and 70 meters wide. (The Great Wall of China is only six meters wide).

And I saw no temple in the city, for its temple is the Lord God the Almighty and the Lamb. And the city has no need of sun or moon to shine on it, for the glory of God gives it light, and its lamp is the Lamb. By its light will the nations walk, and the kings of the earth will bring their glory into it, and its gates will never be shut by day—and there will be no night there. Then the angel showed me the river of the water of life, bright as crystal, flowing from the throne of God and of the Lamb through the middle of the street of the city; also, on either side of the river, the tree of life with its twelve kinds of fruit, yielding its fruit each month. The leaves of the tree were for the healing of the nations.... (Revelation 21:10-22:5)

This is a living temple. The city is filled with people of God and is alive with God himself. It pulses and breaths the Spirit-fed worship of God and of the Lamb:

You also, like living stones, are being built into a spiritual house to be a holy priesthood, offering spiritual sacrifices acceptable to God through Jesus Christ....But you are a chosen people, a royal priesthood, a holy nation, God's special possession, that you may declare the praises of him who called you out of darkness into his wonderful light. (2 Peter 2:5-9)

The New Jerusalem—a complex, harmonious composite

The city is a bride. "Come, I will show you the Bride, the wife of the Lamb."

The New Jerusalem is both city and temple: *"And I saw no temple in the city, for its temple is the Lord God the Almighty and the Lamb"* (Revelation 21:22). There is no temple in this city because this city is a temple—the ultimate temple in which God dwells forever with his people.

This city is made up of many peoples and languages. It is a new world of believers redeemed from every nation: *"By its light will the nations walk, and the kings of the earth will bring their glory into it." (Revelation 21:24)*

This is the ultimate destiny of Christ's church:

> But you are fellow citizens with the saints and members of the household of God, built on the foundation of the apostles and prophets, Christ Jesus himself being the cornerstone, in whom the whole structure, being joined together, grows into a holy temple in the Lord. In him you also are being built together into a dwelling place for God by the Spirit. (Ephesians 2:18-20)

The city is creation restored. From the city center, the original garden river of Eden is restored and eternally perfected. Nourishment, cleansing, and healing are in its waters. Trees of life bend with fruit for the taking.

What hope is found in this heavenly picture! The day will arrive soon. It will be a wedding feast of cosmic proportion. The temple and city will forever be one. Every nation will declare the fame of God. God's church will be victorious and at rest. All who gaze at this vision and pray for its fulfillment grow bold in prayer with the confident assurance that God's kingdom purposes are even now being fulfilled.

The central role of kingdom-come prayer in realizing this vision

In this new Jerusalem, the whole world is born again, a "palingenesis" of heaven and earth. This is the work and ultimate purpose of Christ, our king. Our prayers are like seeds sown in the soil of this broken world, sprouting and growing even now. One day they will bear everlasting fruit. Our prayers and our labors will be taken up into the heavenly vision.

KINGDOM-COME PRAYER TODAY

1. "We become what we pray." How can we pray into these visions?

2. We are called to build a house of prayer. How many "foreigners" are there in your community? How can we open the doors of the church to let them stream in?

3. What will it look like if God fulfills Isaiah 58 and uses you to be a minister of justice and a rebuilder of ancient walls?

4. God is putting watchmen on the walls. Take your place on the walls. Begin to pray. Learn to pray without ceasing for church and city.

5. Pray the sequence in Zechariah, first personally and then on behalf of the church.

6. Think of Ezekiel's river of the Spirit. Dive into the cleansing, healing, and supernatural waters of the Spirit.

7. Big visions require big prayers. The vision in Revelation 21 is the biggest vision of all. It calls for mighty prayers of faith. What are some ways we can pray into this vision?

Appendices

Ten Steps Forward

How to Implement Kingdom Prayer For Church and City

Through a simple prayer in a monastery garden I was converted at the age of seventeen. Soon after I traveled to Denmark, the land of my ancestors, and from Denmark I went to Switzerland and skied until I exhausted my limited resources.

I was encouraged to visit the international headquarters of Youth for Christ in Geneva, and though I was sure they would point me to some great gospel work in a remote destination, they instead pointed me up the Swiss Alps to a little community called L'Abri.

This was my first encounter with prayer as a way of life. The Christian community of L'Abri embodied prayer. Prayer permeated and empowered L'Abri from stem to stern. Every Monday morning we would gather to pray for two hours.

Before and after each meal we prayed meaty prayers. Leaders enveloped their teachings with prayer. A good number came to attend Sunday evening prayer meetings. House leaders set aside one day each month for extended prayer and fasting. And I joined a group of young men who were schooled in prayer practices.

The presence of God was an unquestionable reality. The fellowship in prayer would often break our hearts with affection for God and each other. A sense of purpose pervaded each day and each meeting. People were birthed into Christ, and they were birthed into prayer.

Over the years, others have taught me to pray, either expressly or by example (Jack Miller and Archie Parrish among them).

The following "steps forward" in kingdom prayer narrate practices I have learned from others, received at L'Abri, or administered at Grace Church Vancouver.

These steps forward embody some of our prayer practices and principles over the past thirty years of bringing kingdom prayer into the artery of churches and cities.

They are not a recipe for prayer. Nor are they a formula. There is no "prayer plan" that guarantees kingdom advance and expansion. Rather, the delights of prayer are its individual, organic, spontaneous, and combustive elements. As each person prays, he discovers for himself new joys in the adventure of following Christ in a living way. When one learns to wait upon God in prayer, she discovers fresh wisdom and timely insight hitherto unknown. To mimic any strategy guarantees a stale, second-hand approach.

At the same time, while avoiding formulas, there are proven practices to aid our prayer commitment, and it is often helpful to borrow ideas and strategies to get started. As long as these approaches are simply "training wheels," they can be very helpful.

1. Form your plans in prayer.

First of all, take God at his word that he will let you in on his plan for your life and mission:

Commit your plans to him and he will guide your steps.
(Proverbs 16:3)

Woe to him who makes a plan but not by me/ makes an alliance but not by my Spirit....in repentance and rest is your strength.... He waits to be gracious to those who wait for him....He will say here is the path, walk in it. (Isaiah 30)

In prayer, learn to live supernaturally. Just-in-time revelations of his call and purpose will be given as you read his Word, letting "the word of Christ dwell richly within," and waiting in prayer. May God give you a spirit of wisdom and revelation in the knowledge of him, that the eyes of your heart might be enlightened, that you may know the power.... (Ephesians 1:17ff)

Listening to God and partnering with him was Jesus' method and should be ours:

So Jesus said to them, "Truly, truly, I say to you, the Son can do nothing of his own accord, but only what he sees the Father doing. For whatever the Father does, that the Son does likewise. For the Father loves the Son and shows him all that he himself is doing. And greater works than these will he show him, so that you may marvel. (John 5:19ff)

Have personal and corporate days of "prayer and planning" engaging with God in a rhythm of prayer, the Word, and sharing.

2. Build a prayer centered church and mission by keeping prayer at the center flowing outward.

Bring people to prayer. Call people to specific gatherings and seasons of prayer, such as prayer meetings, prayer vigils, fasting and prayer, and prayer training opportunities.

Just as important: *Bring prayer to the people* so that prayer is increased among people in every area – where prayer acts as a lifeblood that permeates and animates every aspect of mission and ministry. Train every leader to lead their people and ministry area in prayer (see #6 and #7).

This leads to a praying church who exudes a praying culture, where every person is engaged in prayer no matter what their current commitment to prayer is – whether a newcomer on Sunday at the hospitality table or prayer altar after service, to a small group member during Bible study, to a key leader during a planning meeting.

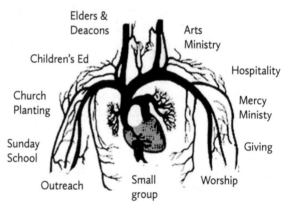

The Christian human rights group International Justice Mission (IJM) sets a powerful example of weaving habits of prayer into their daily practices. Every staff member spends the first 30 minutes of the workday in silence—for prayer, meditation, and spiritual reflection. IJM also gathers staff for 30 minutes of daily corporate prayer, in addition to hosting quarterly offsite spiritual retreats and providing employees with an annual day for private spiritual retreat.

The C2C church planting network has implemented a daily prayer for mission advance by setting their cell phone alarms at 10:02 as a call to prayer. This reminds them throughout their days of Matthew 10:2, to 'Therefore pray earnestly to the Lord of the harvest to send out laborers into his harvest.'

3. Move prayer meetings from boredom to adventure.

Prayer meetings can quickly become stagnant, subject to monotony, and vulnerable to poor attendance. It doesn't have to be this way. Vibrant kingdom prayer can be kept fresh by keeping prayer clusters small—only two to four people.

Encourage participants to pray briefly but often; the acronym ABC (audible, brief, conversational and Christ-centered) is a helpful guide.

Goal of Thirds

Begin the prayer time with a brief Scripture discussion, and practice the Goal of Thirds: one-third instruction, one-third interaction, one-third intercession. Reserve personal requests for the end of the prayer session; pray for the church and city first.

Turn every meeting into a prayer meeting by applying the **Goal of Thirds.** Bringing prayer into the agenda of every meeting transforms them by the presence of Jesus—bringing unity to divided agendas in board meetings, hope to hospital visitations, heart transformation to Sunday school lessons.

Turn every conversation into one that actively invites God in. Model and practice "on the spot" prayer in all settings. This will help people get used to praying with anyone anytime. Instead of saying, "I will pray for you," begin to say, "May I pray for you now?"

4. Practice corporate embodiments of prayer.

Praying with others is supremely helpful. Vision for God's kingdom germinates in the soil of concerted, united prayer. Corporate prayer is the soil in which vision from God grows from mustard seed to mighty plant, providing shade and shelter for many.

Moreover, we need to learn to "embody" our prayers: to stand up, speak out loud, gather in a group, and pray in a circle. These are some of the many ways to move prayer from interior to exterior, from head to heart, from church to city.

5. Incorporate prayer walking into spiritual rhythms.

By far, one of the most important "prayer embodiments" is prayer walking. As you walk the streets of your neighborhood or city, you begin to see things from Jesus' perspective.

One creative example of prayer walking involved mission leaders who arranged a one-day prayer walk of the entire metroplex of Miami, Florida. This group of leaders rode the train from north to south Miami, stopping at every major station along the way to form a prayer circle. One of the leaders from that area would narrate the needs and opportunities of that community, pointing out essential landmarks and institutions. In this way, they prayed for the specific neighborhoods of the entire city in detail and "on location."

6. Choose leaders who are committed to prayer and train them to pray.

We become what we pray. Choose, appoint, elect, or hire people who are excited to be part of a praying team. Before long, prayer will advance and inform the entire culture of your enterprise.

When examining potential leaders spend as much time exploring their prayer life and practices as their proficiency in teaching and pastoring. Ask about their personal prayer practices.

Ensure that all nominees for office take a basic training prayer course before being placed before the congregation for voting.

Prayer will be pushed to the margins unless recognized officers and leaders provide the example of a godly life of intercession for the church and world. Choose your strongest leaders to train others in prayer.

Likewise, train your congregational prayer leaders how to lead in prayer, so that public prayer projects weight and meaning rather than just a laundry list of health problems and news-related issues. Leading with the Lord's Prayer or other psalm or Scripture ensures the vitality of congregational prayer.

Make sure to provide basic prayer training before asking someone to lead in prayer, just as you would if asking someone to teach or lead a Bible study. Debrief prayer leadership just as you would debrief a sermon or Bible study.

Another important way to multiply prayer leadership and to care for the flock is to implement prayer visitation. Train several leaders and leader couples in how to minister to the members of a flock in prayer. Paul the apostle provides a stellar example of ministering in prayer, as he prayed 64 times for the churches. (see chapter 6). The time-honored practice of regular elder visitation can be updated by sending a mature couple to pray for each household. Whenever an individual, couple or family is going through hard times, send a team to pray for them.

7. Train small group leaders to be prayer leaders.

When the ethos of small groups embodies vibrant prayer, every meeting becomes a prayer meeting, and organic prayer begins to form the bedrock of your church. Every small group leader can be trained to become a prayer leader.

Provide small groups the pattern of equal parts fellowship, study, and prayer. At Grace Vancouver Church we encouraged people to enjoy dinner together, then move into a season of praise and thanksgiving, followed by a brief Bible study, with lots of discussion and application.

The stage would thus be set for informed prayer for others and one another. In order to balance inward and outward concerns, the prayer time would begin with praying for the church and the city. After this we would field personal requests and pray for one another.

8. Implement seasons of "waiting prayer" into the calendar.

By "waiting prayer" we mean designated seasons of prayer and fasting, similar to the first disciples' waiting for the promised Holy Spirit as Jesus commanded them. In the case of Grace Vancouver, for example, we started our church plant with sixteen weeks of prayer meetings.

Once the church began, we would continue to gather weekly for two hours of prayer and reporting.

Three times a year, we held a day of prayer and fasting, and every fall we gathered all our ministry leaders together for a day of prayer and planning. These prayer times were not only times of preparation; they were highpoints of spiritual joy and team building.

9. Form prayer evangelism triads.

To encourage people in personal mission and evangelism, establish a network of prayer-evangelism triads, in which each participant chooses three non-Christian friends or neighbors to pray for. Triads gather regularly to pray for one another's lives and outreach. Each person in the triad shares according to three questions to focus prayers:

1. How are you growing in your prayer friendship with Jesus?
2. How are you connecting with your friends in acts of kind and words of wisdom?
3. How can we best pray for them, and for your opportunities to love and serve them?

Once the group has strong cohesion and clear purpose, one or two members will leave to form a new triad. The goal is to have every member and faithful attender become part of a prayer triad. The original group members keep in touch with each other to maintain friendship and encourage the process.

10. Discover and adopt mottos for prayer advance.

Over the years, we have assembled a collection of mottos that inspire us to prioritize prayer. We keep these front and center to instill an ongoing culture of kingdom prayer.

Here are some of our favourites:

We are what we pray.

We become what we pray.

We either pray it open or we pry it open.

There is no cruise control with prayer.

Pray or be prey.

We do not pray for revival. Prayer is revival.

Spiritual warfare does not follow prayer. Prayer is spiritual warfare.

As in all things, pray about how God wants you to lead and grow in the endeavor of kingdom prayer.

Here is a simple sequence of prayer as a way to focus on one priority of the Lord's prayer at a time. Pray through one priority (i.e. one column) from top to bottom at a time.

1. Upward (PATTERN & PRIORITY)		Day 1
• Start your prayer by focusing on the priority **upward to God.** • **Praise** Jesus for the priority.	**PATTERN**	Our **Father** in heaven
• **Meditate** on the priority. Ask the Holy Spirit to show you **what it means.** What does the priority **tell you about God?**	**PRIORITY**	Relationship Drawing close to God
2. Inward (PASSIONS)	Pray God's **PASSIONS** into my own heart	
• Next pray the priority **into your heart.** Talk with God about it. • How is the priority **growing or lacking** in your heart and life? • **What will your life look like** as this priority takes deeper root? Ask Jesus to **transform your heart** and life to be more like his.		
3. Outward (PEOPLE)	Pray God's blessing for other **PEOPLE**	
• Now pray for **others to experience more of** God's promises and priority in their lives. • Pray for **the world, the church, and the city,** especially as needs relate to the focus priority at hand.		
4. Upward (PRAISE)	**PRAISE** for who he is & answers to my prayers	
• End by **praising God** for his blessings and answers to prayer. **Recognize** how God has been present. **Thank** him.		

For further elaboration on using this prayer sequence/grid, please see Seven Days of
Prayer with Jesus *by John Smed from www.prayercurrent.com*

Day 2	Day 3	Day 4	Day 5	Day 6	Day 7
Our Father, **Holy** is your name	Our Father, **Your kingdom** come	Our Father, **Your will** be done	Our Father, Give us this day our **daily bread**	Our Father, **Forgive us** as we forgive our debtors	Our Father, **Lead us** not into temptation, deliver us
Worship Joyfully Obeying	Proclaiming the kingdom Sharing Jesus	Opening up and trusting God's direction	Thanksgiving Contentment Simplicity	Humility & trust to let go Unity	Commitment to the Kingdom Guidance Advance

There are practical ways we can encourage intercession for our land. One way to pray effectively for your country is to pray for the nation in the same way you pray for a person. Take a flip chart and divide it into four quadrants. In each corner write one of these four questions:

 LOVE:

What do you **LOVE** about your country?

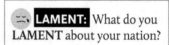 **LAMENT:** What do you **LAMENT** about your nation?

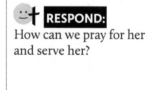 **REPENT:** What **IDOLS** and **SINS** grieve you (and God) about your country?

RESPOND:
How can we pray for her and serve her?

Next, have the group discuss and write down their answers to these questions.

For quadrant one, think and pray about why you love the nation God where has placed you (see Acts 17:26-28) and write down your answers.

For quadrant two, discussing the hurts and brokenness, consider the different ways Satan and sin are wounding and oppressing.

In the third quadrant, write down the nation's sins and the idols that will bring judgment if not repented of.

In the last quadrant, write down the prayers and actions God is calling you to enact for your land.

LOVE her Beauty	**LAMENT over Brokenness**
Work-life balance	*Hyper sexualized*
Health, wellness, fitness, yoga	*Port city brings drug trade &*
Beauty of nature	*Human trafficking*
Environmental Sustainability	*Disconnection & distraction*
Diversity, open-minded	*Superficiality*
Multicultural	*Loneliness*
Community development	*Mental health struggles*
Spiritual, seeking purpose/good	*Addictions*
Key industries: tourism & film	*Poverty, disparity of wealth*
REPENT for her Idols	**RESPOND in prayer & mission**
LEISURE/PLEASURE	*Jesus gave up all pleasures of heaven,*
	approval of his father and submitted to
Approval, acceptance, tolerance	*the cross for us to receive ultimate riches*
Power, Self-sufficiency	*and approval.*
Purpose	*Speak God's story, film outreach*
	Creation care, outdoors ministries
	Social justice, serving the poor
	Prayer evangelism

This exercise can be adapted for a nation, city or neighborhood. This is a sample quadrant completed for Vancouver, Canada, a West Coast city.

Once the chart is complete, have the group take an extended time to pray for your country, one quadrant at a time.

The entire process should take less than an hour.

If you have a larger number joining you in prayer, divide the group into teams of five or eight, then let each group fill out the quadrants and pray for the country. After each team is finished praying, pass the sheet on to the next group, or have the groups walk aroun the room to different tables, so you can see how others care about their country—and pray again.

Of course, if several nations are represented, all the better! You can pray for countries around the world this way. Circumnavigate the globe through kingdom prayer!

This exercise can also be used to pray for cities, neighbourhoods, and people groups.

Select Bibliography

Beeke, Joel R., and Brian G. Najapfour, editors. 2011. *Taking Hold of God: Reformed and Puritan Perspectives on Prayer*. Grand Rapids, MI: Reformation Heritage/Soli Deo Gloria.

Bloesch, Donald G. 1988. *The Struggle of Prayer*. Colorado Spring, CO: Helmers & Howard.

Carson, D. A. 2002. *Teach us to Pray: Prayer in the Bible and in the World*. Eugene, OR: Wipf and Stock.

Hand, Thomas A, editor. 1963. *Saint Augustine on Prayer*. Newman House Press.

Hayes, Dan. 2009. *Fireseeds of Spiritual Awakening: Igniting the Flame of Spiritual Renewal*. Orlando, FL: Cru Press.

Houston, James. 2010. *Transforming Friendship: A Guide to Prayer*. Vancouver: Regent Press.

Jeffries, David Lyle, editor. Third edition 2006. *A Burning and a Shining light: English Spirituality in the Age of Wesley*. Vancouver: Regent Press.

Keller, Timothy. 2012. *Center Church: Doing Balanced, Gospel-Centered Ministry in Your City*. Grand Rapids, MI: Zondervan.

McIntyre, David. 2010. *The Hidden Life of Prayer: The Life-blood of the Christian*. Plantation, FL: Fowler Digital Books. Originally published in 1891.

Murray, Andrew. 2003. *The Ministry of Intercessory Prayer*. Bloomington, MN: Bethany House.

Spurgeon, Charles. *The Power of Prayer in a Believers Life*. Lynwood, Washington. Emerald Books. Compiled 1993.